THE FEAR OF FAILURE

HOW TO BECOME AN ACTION TAKER, STOP WORRYING, OVERCOME PROCRASTINATION AND PERFECTIONISM

WILDA HALE

CONTENTS

Just for you!
A FREE GIFT

As a way to thank you for your purchase, you will be getting the "12 tips & tricks to help you become a better and faster decision maker" eBook for free :) Click HERE to access your gift or go to www.wildahale.com

INTRODUCTION

Franklin Roosevelt, the 32nd president of the United States, said:

"The only thing we have to fear is fear itself."

Most often, fear holds us back more than any obstacle would.

I've wasted many years of my life and a tremendous amount of opportunities due to my insecurities, overthinking, not feeling ready or good enough. This constant self-doubt in my abilities made me feel imprisoned, hopeless, and miserable.

I used to look at all the extraordinary people of this world and think that maybe they are made differently. Maybe there's something special about them. Perhaps just a few chosen ones have been born to be great and been given the ideal circumstances in life. But not me. I didn't think I had what it takes. I felt that all the odds are against me. I thought success and greatness in life were reserved for others. And this type of thinking did nothing but keep me stuck in a life that I hated for a long time.

It took me a while until I saw that in reality, people are not very different from one another. Fundamentally, we are all the same. But, if we're all so similar, then what differentiates the successful ones from those that lead a mediocre existence? Is it opportunities? Talent? Is it luck? Or intelligence?

Well, I won't deny that these factors definitely have an influence, but it's not what separates the winners from the rest. We all have seen top athletes, celebrities, and top CEOs that do not necessarily come from the best backgrounds and wealthiest families. They're not geniuses either. So, what is it then?

Before answering this question, I want to be clear about what I refer to when I say "successful". I think success is different for everyone. For some, financial success is extremely important, while for others, money might not even be a part of the standards they measure success by. I think those who achieve it are the ones that simply live life on their own terms, fulfilling their purpose.

Now, to answer the question: I think that the differentiating factor is people's attitude towards failure. How we react when encountering an obstacle is what sets us apart.

Kyle Rote once said:

"There is no doubt in my mind that there are many ways to be a winner, but there is really one way to be a loser, and that is to fail and not look beyond failure."

I'm no stranger to failure, and I don't know anyone that hasn't experienced it in one way or another, which is why I felt inspired to write this book. I think people don't talk enough about their shortcomings and downfalls. We love to hear success stories. However, most often, we're not aware of someone's entire journey with all their ups and, more importantly, their downs.

I've failed in friendships. I've failed in romantic relationships. I've also had a few business ventures in my twenties that failed because I allowed my fears to take the best out of me. I would start a business, and after the first few obstacles, I would give up feeling defeated and disappointed. I repeated the same process over and over: started a new business idea, followed by getting stuck and eventually quitting.

It took me several failures until I realized that I got it all wrong. I saw the lack of success as a sign to stop in my journey instead of seeing it as what it really was: feedback.

I don't regret any of my past experiences. And I know it's a cheesy thing to say, but it's the truth — I became grateful for my struggles. They created a hunger that one won't find in comfort. They created pain, disappointment that I had to overcome. Being where I am today provides me with enough strength, encouragement, and experience to know that everything had to happen the way it did.

Inside all humans on this planet, there is the desire to pursue their biggest ambitions. Millions of people dream about being entrepreneurs, painters, writers, actors, therapists; however, instead of following their instincts and dreams, they become complacent in an unfulfilling, mediocre existence. All because that's their comfort zone, and outside of that area, the world looks like a scary place. They are too intimidated by their own goals and of what might happen if they chase them, freezing in the face of potential failures.

Fear is normal, and it should be expected in challenging situations. Still, the moment it starts to be so debilitating that it hinders you from even trying to achieve your goals, it has to be dealt with as soon as possible.

The fear of failure is one of the most common fears. According to a survey conducted by Linkagoal, 31% of 1,083 adults fear failure, more than those who fear spiders or being home alone. So many are afraid to live...

You convince yourself that it's ok to have a dull existence, simply for the fact that it feels safer! You get scared that a potential failure could result in financial distress or negatively affect your personal relations. While staying in the comfort zone gives you a feeling of security, this fear only ends up taking away opportunities and experiences in the long term.

The most common indicators of the fear of failure are:

- lack of action due to extreme perfectionism
- self-doubt
- overthinking
- procrastination

When you fear failure, you will often ask yourself questions like "What if I'll embarrass myself?" or "What if others will think that I'm stupid?".

There will be a tendency to avoid taking more important responsibilities at work or school, worrying you will disappoint. This behavior will only keep you stuck in life. While you are shielded from failures, you miss out on the best that life has to offer.

By all means, do the best you can to prepare for what's in front of you. Making informed decisions and being cautious is necessary. However, after a certain point, trying to prevent failure does more harm than any mistake ever could.

What is *wrong* teaches us what is *right*. Before having any achievement, athletes have to spend thousands of hours training. Children have to practice riding a bike. Doctors need years of study and practice before being able to do their job well. The process itself is not fun. Children will fall off their bikes and scrape their knees when learning. Athletes will be defeated throughout their careers, and even experienced doctors will make mistakes. Like it or not, life is imperfect, and we need to learn to roll with the punches. The unknown, mistakes, risks, and failures are all part of it.

Within the pages of this book, you will learn:

- Where your fears originate from and how to overcome them
- To redefine your perspective on failure
- About some of the most successful people and how they handled their failures
- How to swap perfectionism for progress
- How to become an action taker instead of an overthinker
- How to stop self-sabotaging and conquer your procrastination tendencies
- How to increase your motivation to get more done
- Great ways to manage your stress and gain inner peace

- To desensitize yourself from the pain of rejection
- To stop accepting less than you deserve
- To become a happier version of yourself

I want you to get out of your own way. I understand how it feels when the voice inside your head always looks for a way to hold you back. But it's about time you start nurturing a new voice: one that reminds you that you're good enough and that encourages you to push through when all seems to fall apart.

How many times have you missed out on something that could have changed your life, all because you were too afraid? When is the last time you let yourself take a chance? Can you recall a time when you celebrated your own growth?

Self-doubt and imagining the worst-case scenario can make us feel broken, but the scars that form after healing from it are not ugly. They become badges of strong willpower and motivation.

How to make the most of this read?

If you want to get the most out of this book, make sure you:

- Have a sincere desire to make improvements to your life — this is the number one requirement. Don't read it in a hurry. Take the time to understand and then put into use the information you read after each chapter. If you wait to read the entire book before implementing the techniques and action steps, you will have information overload. It is one of the most common problems people have when reading a book or taking a course. It's why so many find it challenging to apply the knowledge to their lives, so they end up seeing little to no progress.

- Highlight those paragraphs you find important, so when you revisit this book, you can easily see and remember the main ideas.

- Keep track of your progress on a monthly basis. Check what mistakes you are still making, what you have learned, and what is yet to be improved.

- You won't be able to implement 100% of the ideas from this book after your first read, and it's perfectly fine. I know this because even if I've written the book myself, I sometimes have trouble applying all the principles. It takes time and practice to form better habits. It's an imperfect process — sometimes you will do better, sometimes you will do worse. My recommendation for you is to keep this book handy and go over the chapters as many times as you will feel necessary.

"*It is impossible to live without failing at something unless you live so cautiously that you might as well not have lived at all, in which case you have failed by default.*"

— J.K. ROWLING

1

UNDERSTANDING FEAR

"The mind is a powerful force. It can enslave us or empower us. It can plunge us into the depths of misery or take us to the heights of ecstasy. Learn to use the power wisely."

— DAVID CUSCHIERI

The human brain is one of the most complex things in the entire Universe, and you get to own one – how wonderful is that?

You don't have to be a psychiatrist to be curious about your mind. If you want to better manage your mindset, you need to understand what's going on inside that pretty head of yours.

Ultimately, knowledge gives us control over how to use our brains' incredible power and leads the way towards a healthy mindset. But first, let's understand what exactly fear is, respectively the fear of failure.

We've all got to know fear in some moment of our lives. While generally considered a "negative" emotion, it serves an essential role in keeping us safe. Fear is a survival mechanism, and its purpose is to alert us to the presence of a threat or danger.

Fear always involves two kinds of responses in our bodies:

1. a *biochemical response*
2. an *emotional response*

The biochemical (physical) response is universal. It is also called the "fight or flight" response, which means the body is prepared to either enter combat or run away. This automatic reaction is crucial for our survival. When we feel a particular threat, it kick-starts the processes needed to defend us against danger. Cortisol is released into our body, increasing our heart rate, focusing our attention, and regulating our breathing.

No matter if our stressor is mental or physical, we will still have the same biochemical reaction.

When you fear failure, the automatic flight response comes into action. The stressor is the task that needs to be completed. Rather than dealing with it or getting it done, it's easier to run away from it. Hence, you never have to experience a potential failure.

The emotional response is personalized, as it varies from individual to individual, unlike the biochemical response. So, there are people who are adrenaline seekers, thriving on fear-inducing thrill situations, and on the other side of the spectrum, there are those who avoid fear-inducing situations.

Even if the physical reaction is the same, the experience of fear is perceived as good or bad, depending on each person.

Our core fears

When we avoid something, it could also mean avoiding the debilitating or fatal consequences that happen after. The negative aftermath we are afraid of is the source of pain and fear.

According to the author and lecturer Dr. Karl Albrecht, there are **five core fears** we all share:

1. Extinction
2. Mutilation
3. Loss of autonomy
4. Separation
5. Ego death (Albrecht, 2012)

1. The fear of extinction refers to our fear of losing our existence. It is essentially our fear of dying. Our body is wired to help us survive. Let's say you're walking and all of a sudden you trip. Your body is naturally wired to grab onto something to prevent you from falling; at the very least, you put your hands out to keep your face from smacking into the pavement. Your body tells you not to eat something that smells or looks funny, as it might make you sick. You shield your eyes when something gets thrown your way. We are naturally wired to ensure we do not die, which is why this is the most common and obvious fear.

2. The fear of mutilation refers to our desire to protect our bodies. We get scared of spiders and snakes because they could harm us physically. On an emotional level, we fear someone hurting us or violating our boundaries.

3. Loss of autonomy is the fear we will lose control. It's not that we naturally want to be powerful; we simply seek control over ourselves to ensure our safety and protection.

4. Our fear of **separation** reveals we don't want to be abandoned. Everyone wants to feel like a part of a group, as it helps to secure our social status and prevent us from loneliness.

5. Finally, our fear of humiliation, also called the fear of **ego-death,** refers to the idea that we want to prevent ourselves from embarrassment. No one wants to be humiliated. We want to feel valuable, capable, and worthy of love.

By understanding our deepest, most animalistic fears, it's easier to evaluate why we might have such anxiety even over the most seemingly harmless situation.

For example, think about how nervous you felt before an exam. If you had failed, it could have resulted in you flunking college, meaning you wouldn't have been able to get a job. Later on, you won't be able to make ends meet and support yourself, finally tracing back to the fear of extinction. Also, you might have had a fear of ego-death because you worried that your classmates/ family/ friends would have judged you if you failed. Using these core fears helps to lay out what it is that is truly scaring us.

Childhood and failure

Children with an early established fear of failure might view learning negatively and even cheat on assignments. Rather than focusing on what is best for them, they place precedence on validating their ego .

(British Psychological Society, 2014)

From such a young age, many of us were set up to evaluate situations with the fear of failure in mind. Considering these childhood effects, we can start to dismantle the long-lasting impact that's still present today.

The first place to start is with your parents, peers, and anyone else who contributed to your development throughout childhood. Our parents can set us up for failure by being overprotective, emotionally abusive, or simply ignoring our needs.

You might have been a child whose parents never let you fail in the first place. Challenge, disappointment, and other adversities are a natural part of life; if children are never given the opportunity to experience them, they are robbed of the chance to grow from these mistakes.

Any parent would tell you they want to protect their child. Unfortunately, many parents don't know how to do that in the best way possible, so they become overprotective; letting children fail means allowing them to recognize the scale of their own autonomy. They begin to understand their abilities and how decisions made now can affect things later. Some lessons can only be learned through mistakes. When that opportunity gets taken away, it makes the inevitable failure we face later in life so much harder to manage. When children have been sheltered from adversity their entire existence, they are at a higher risk of developing depression later on. They are robbed of the chance to learn from natural consequences that would eventually help them develop high levels of competence.

Your parents might have sheltered you if they completed homework assignments for you or did your chores, meaning you had to put in little effort for your development. Though they might have been trying to help or make your life more enjoyable, they were also putting in the hard work that provides you with gratification later on.

Even if your parents weren't overprotective, they might've had a negative impact on your development if they bullied you without realizing it by laughing at some of your mistakes or shamed you any time you messed up. If they were always ready to snap at every little slip-up, it could make performing any task scary now. Let's say you had to do the dishes but accidentally broke a plate in the process – if your parent screamed at you in response, it could make doing any chore feel quite stressful. If you got punished for bad grades or if you've been embarrassed at school for getting something wrong, most probably that left a mark on you. What if you mess up again? Even as adults, we can still hear that voice in the back of our heads, making us feel scared.

Moving beyond our programming

It's very likely you have a smartphone on you right now. Most mobile phones have between 32 and 64 GB of memory space available. From pictures to texts to 1,000 unread spam e-mails, our phones can store a ton of information. While it might seem like a lot when you're holding such a small device, what's even more incredible is the amount of storage in your brain: roughly *one million GB of storage* available. It can seem difficult to change your thoughts around, but information like this reminds us just how capable we are to alter the way our mind works.

Your thoughts are malleable and undoubtedly capable of change. Remember that you could watch TV for 300 years straight and still have extra room in your memory (Reber, 2010).

What exists in your mind can be transformed; all you need is a real desire to do so and small, consistent changes.

Become more aware of your thoughts and where they are coming from. Finding the root of the problem makes it easier to dig it out and remove it, so it doesn't come back. Did someone else put a certain thought in your head? Is there a repeated thought that has followed you from childhood? Evaluate the origin to expose the weakness of it.

Chapter 1: Key Takeaways

1. Fear acts as a survival mechanism, and its purpose is to alert us about the presence of a threat. Fear creates two types of responses in our bodies: the physical reaction, which is the same for everyone, and the emotional reaction, which is different for every individual.

2. The physical reaction is also called the "fight or flight" response, where we choose to either enter combat or run away. Those who fear failure decide to run from the stressor to avoid any possible negative results.

3. Parents, peers, or other people who contributed to your development during childhood greatly influence how you perceive failure later in life. Both overprotective parents and extremely critical ones can have a negative impact. Letting children fail is necessary. They need to understand their abilities, learn to push through, and see failure as part of life instead of perceiving it negatively.

Some lessons can only be learned through mistakes. When that opportunity gets taken away, it makes the inevitable failure we face later in life much more difficult to manage. When a child has been sheltered from adversity their entire life, they will face a high risk of developing depression later on.

CHANGING YOUR PERSPECTIVE

"Success is not final; failure is not fatal. It is the courage to continue that counts"

— WINSTON CHURCHILL

*N*o two humans think alike – even identical twins. We are all individuals who have experienced very different things in our lives. How we were raised, what we were taught to believe, the media we consumed, and the people we surrounded ourselves with ended up shaping our attitudes. All these influencing sources carry a different perspective, so added together, the results are always going to vary.

Some things are seen as "bad" by society, and failure is one of them. Though this perception has been reiterated in our culture so frequently, who says we can't change it?

The perspective we have on failure can often be the thing that keeps us continually making mistakes. It's not just me stating this, but also the experts that studied the psychology of failure.

A study was made a few years ago on a number of people who wanted to diet. They have been split into two groups, and all have been fed the same size slice of pizza. Afterwards, the participants were given cookies to taste, but they were not given a specific amount this time. They were allowed to eat as many as they wanted.

Something very interesting was observed by those who conducted the study: *the group which perceived the slice of pizza as big ended up eating more cookies than the group who believed the slices were small.* The participants that thought they had ruined their diet were more likely to give in to that temptation which the cookies presented, ignoring their dietary regime in the process. Those who didn't think they had made any mistakes ended up choosing not to self-sabotage when tempted again (Deo, Herman, Polivy, 2010).

Research like this reminds us that even when we fail, we don't have to let that be the end of the road. All those dieters ate the same size slice of pizza. *Simply feeling like they failed the first time led to more destructive decisions.*

We can assume this also indicates the more we succeed, the more we are likely to make good decisions.

Our perspective on success is that you can either have one or the other. You're either the best or the worst. Limited thinking like this leads us to act in a predictable way. You gave in and had pizza for lunch, so you may as well have fast food for dinner. You already missed your work deadline, so you may as well give up on the project. These thoughts perpetuate a cycle of unhealthy failure.

You have to become more aware of this type of behavior. It's normal not to give 100% on each and every occasion. If you start exercising and miss a day, that doesn't mean you should give it up — every little effort matters. Get out of the mindset that things will come to you "eventually". Saving half of your sandwich for later is a small way to promote a healthy mindset when dieting. Choosing not to buy one shirt is enough to save some extra money when you're working on your finances. Not every step towards growth will be a huge leap. Sometimes those tiny steps add up to more than the big jumps. Not only do small risks help you improve, but they lead to small failures. Regrouping after smaller mistakes is much easier than after the big ones.

But why do we think failure is wrong in the first place? Fundamentally, we are group animals; this means we have a dependency on others for survival. Think of a lion pride. The hunters go out at night to kill, while some stay back to protect the cubs.

Back in our tribal days, humans had a similar system. Some were strong enough to go out and hunt bison, pigs, and other prey for dinner. Some took care of the children, and others planted food.

Because of this necessity for others, it is natural to want to be accepted by the "group". Our self-esteem is heightened when we feel valuable, have a purpose, and hold a position.

Life today, though, allows for much more independence: you can go to the store and get your food, you can hire a nanny to take care of the kids, or someone to clean your home. However, there are different pressures to fit in with society now. Having a group of friends keeps you entertained and prevents you from loneliness. A spouse or life partner allows you to create a family. Having a strong network in your career means more opportunities for success.

Failing could mean becoming an outcast. What if we'll be judged? What if someone doesn't want to work with us? What if we get broken up with or cast out of our group of friends?

Failure creates insecurity. What if we aren't good enough? What if we lose our job? What if we can't afford to pay our bills?

Fearing failure isn't just insecurity because we want to be liked by others. It's a survival instinct. At the end of the day, our animalistic brains just want to keep us alive.

It's essential to understand the only person we should worry about letting down is ourselves. Even if we fail big, people won't leave us, and if they do, then maybe they weren't the right ones to have in our lives in the first place.

Fearing failure might feel natural, but we can work on overcoming it.

The Iceberg of Success

Icebergs are seemingly small lumps of ice on the top of the surface. However, what's underneath is a massive structure.

When looking at success, you could describe it the same way as an iceberg. It's easy to see the success someone has had, but underneath all of that, there is so much more. What's beneath the surface is a lot of mistakes, dedication, failure, persistence, and disappointment that helped to build that achievement. Under the surface is criticism. Critical comments or judgments from others could make us want to stop; it might feel like they're validating all the bad things we think of ourselves.

Everyone saw Michael Phelps win 28 Olympic gold medals. What we didn't see were the 6-day training weeks that led up to this. The sacrifices that he made.

The tip of the iceberg is everything that is seen most often. As David Perell said:

"We see the success, but not the hard work. We see trophies, not sweat. We see diplomas, not homework. We see performances, not rehearsals."

We should let all the mistakes and criticism become a basis for us to grow, instead of something that may stop us.

Destination: Success

A lot of us expect success to be a perfect upward progression. Now you are down, but tomorrow you will be up, right? Yeah... not really. It's more like a roller coaster of ups and downs. Sometimes we might hit a super high point in our achievements but then plateau for a while. We might dip down lower than we have before, but like a pendulum, we can swing just as high the opposite way.

Failure will feel less intimidating after each fall. Think of it like working out. The first time you go to the gym after three years of never exercising is going to cause pain the next day. However, each day you go back, it's going to hurt a little less. After a couple of months, it no longer hurts to work out, and you'll be stronger than before.

Failure is terrifying because our minds wander to the deepest, darkest places. Even if we went through the worst-case scenario, we would still find a way to recover. Your most embarrassing moments might still sting a little when you start to think of them, but you probably lived through a lot more than you can even remember.

Learn from Jeff

Do you think the creator of Pets.com regrets starting the business? It launched in 1999, eventually failing in 2002. What about the creator of MyHabit or Askville? You might not be familiar with these because, like Pets.com, they also failed after brief periods. Besides the fact that all of these are failed businesses, the one thing these websites have in common is that they all came from the great mind of Jeff Bezos — the founder of the multi-billion-dollar company, Amazon!

One of the richest men in the world, Jeff Bezos is no stranger to failure. He claims to have lost billions from failed business ideas, some of them including:

- Amazon TestDrive
- Amazon Local Register
- Amazon Wallet
- Amazon Fire Phone

Amazon lost an astonishing 170 million dollars on the Fire Phone. However, Jeff Bezos still told his development leader not to lose a minute of sleep over the massive failure. (Clifford, 2020)

Jeff Bezos believes expecting to fail is a liberating experience (Woods, 2018). When he started Amazon in his garage, that was just the beginning of a long journey that led him to be one of the world's wealthiest men. What used to be a website for books has turned into a hundred-billion-dollar company. He makes more in a minute than most households make in a year ($150,000 on average).

While not every company, endeavor, or even risk will result in a fortune like Amazon's, it's a perfect example of how failure can lead to greater success. What if he had decided to call it quits after the first failure?

Before becoming the CEO of his own company, Bezos worked as the senior vice president for D.E. Shaw. He could have kept his position and still would have lived a life more successful than most. However, *he only saw failure as a way to push forward.*

Bezos claimed he would be more haunted by what he had never finished than by the things he tried and failed. (Samia, n.d.)

There are plenty of success stories out there. I'm hoping for more people to realize that the most remarkable achievements don't come at the first attempt, so taking the time to build experience is essential in any journey. There's a ton of examples of people that failed or saw minimal success in the beginning. Still, because they pushed through, they got to see their dreams become a reality.

Yes, failure can make us feel disappointed, but that it's a temporary thing. On the other hand, never trying to accomplish anything isn't. The potentials in life that have come and passed remain as ghosts that haunt us wherever we go.

Before trying anything, the "what ifs" cycle through your mind nonstop. From there, you have two options. You can try, and then the "what ifs" stop. You got your results, and even if they were terrible, you're able now to move on.

The other option is to stay safe and not take the chance, but you'll never know what might have happened, and these thoughts tend to haunt us for a very long time.

It's important to get comfortable taking risks. They aren't the same as gambling, so don't leave everything up to chance. At the same time, rolling the dice every now and then might give you some of the best results of your life.

Les Brown said:

"The graveyard is the richest place on earth because it is here that you will find all the hopes and dreams that were never fulfilled, the books that were never written, the songs that were never sung, the inventions that were never shared, the cures that were never discovered, all because someone was too afraid to take that first step, keep with the problem, or determined to carry out their dream."

So, please, don't keep your talents, your inventions, your art to yourself. That is selfish. It doesn't do anyone any good. Not to you, not to society. Share it! Believe in it!

A Growth Mindset

The concept of a growth mindset was talked about initially in the book "Mindset: the new psychology of success", written by the American psychologist and professor Carol Dweck. It's not a notion she invented, but a trait she noticed in people who have the most success in life. Eventually, she started to look for ways to help other people develop this attribute.

In her early years as a researcher, Carol Dweck saw that while some children had a positive perspective over obstacles, enjoying challenges, others would perceive difficulties in a negative way.

She believes there are two mindsets people have: the growth mindset and the fixed mindset.

The characteristics of people with fixed mindsets are:

- They think their abilities cannot be changed or developed
- Take critical feedback very personal
- Prefer easier tasks
- Give up easily when facing an obstacle
- See failure as final
- Less likely to take risks
- Will be focused on the outcome and will look to get results as fast as possible
- When failing, they will question their abilities and be quick to think they are not capable enough.

On the other hand, the people with growth mindsets:

- Think they can develop their abilities
- Embrace challenges and change

- Know setbacks aren't permanent roadblocks
- Seek improvement
- Enjoy experimenting and innovating
- Focus on the journey
- Don't see failure as an option; they continuously look to improve and learn, seeing obstacles as opportunities.

The two mindsets will influence so many aspects of one's life, from the willingness to take risks, to how critical feedback is received and whether one will manage to finish difficult tasks.

Having a growth mindset will set you apart from the majority of people. What's most important is that anyone could develop it, so it is not a quality people are just born with.

By wanting to adopt a growth mindset, you're already taking the first step towards letting yourself flourish. It doesn't matter how old you are or what beliefs you held previously. Our minds are constantly growing, and we can nourish them for even greater results.

How can you develop a growth mentality?

1. Through continuous learning

Make sure you continue to educate yourself and keep an open mind. Invest in books, courses, classes, and these efforts will certainly get to know results. Investing in yourself is the best kind of investment you could ever make. We continue to learn throughout our entire lives; it doesn't end by any means the moment we finished our formal education. Knowledge will enable you to come up with new solutions, better ideas and ultimately increase your success.

2. Through perseverance

It's easy that whenever you feel a little bit frustrated, to want to quit. And the truth is most people do it. Discipline yourself to always look at what a challenge will add, not what will take away from you. Don't run from failure. Sometimes we just have to admit that we messed up or we were wrong. It can feel uncomfortable, but only for a moment.

Our worth shouldn't be found in our successes, but rather our ability to continue fighting for success even when it's far away. You will undoubtedly face challenges because it is an integral part of any endeavor that is worth pursuing. During our lowest moments, we develop our strength and character. Challenges build our resiliency, so we're able to face even bigger roadblocks in the future. Yes, the ego dislikes failure because it doesn't want to accept there is more to learn.

Taking action when facing a challenge helps us develop personal responsibility and makes us less susceptible to blaming external factors. The confidence we gain when accomplishing difficult tasks frees up our spirits.

3. By being open to feedback

Being open to feedback is necessary if we want to learn quickly and improve our chances for success. There is nothing as helpful as understanding what is working and what is not.

Not being willing to grow will have a say in your success. A lot of people see criticism as a personal attack. It's hard to hear others' critical opinions, especially when it involves something we put our heart and soul into. However, hearing other people out is a way for us to learn even more.

A large part of this battle will involve believing in yourself. Remember a time when you thought you wouldn't make it through. We all have been through challenges before. Use your past experiences as a reminder that you are capable of growth. Reflect on the important lessons you've learned over time and how they have enabled you to get closer to success.

4. By celebrating other people's successes

To make your journey an enjoyable one, stop comparing yourself and be intimidated by others. Be happy for what they managed to achieve. How you handle other people's success, especially when you might not be doing so well, says a lot about your confidence and level of maturity. Genuinely celebrate others and their achievements. It will bring you a lot of joy and create the right energy to be surrounded with.

Resist jealousy and comparison. A fixed mindset will want to do things just to impress other people or prove them wrong. A person with this mindset follows other people's motives and intentions rather than creating their own. Find a deep meaning inside of yourself for wanting to improve. When you create a passion worth fighting for, this will be your tool against your fear of failure.

Trick your brain and replace fear

Even though fear's primary role is to keep us alert in case of danger, there is no doubt that fear stops us from doing a lot of the things we would like to do. If not dealt with correctly, our own survival mechanisms end up robbing us of so many experiences that we would like to have. For example, if you're scared to ask for a salary raise at your job, that will restrict the amount of money you're making. If you're afraid of asking someone out, that will prevent you from meeting a potential partner. Fear is something that stops most people in an aspect or another of their lives. But it really shouldn't. So, I'm going to share an excellent technique with you that works wonders. I've been using it for a while now, and it made a great difference in my life! I know it will do too in yours. It's so simple but so effective. This method's efficacy has been proved even in studies made at Harvard. They measured individuals' performances when this technique was used compared to when it wasn't, and clear improvements were seen as a result of it.

Before I tell you what this method is about and how you can implement it into your life, let me share some facts about fear that you probably haven't been aware of until now.

The feelings of fear and excitement have more in common than you might have realized. *They are both aroused emotions, with <u>the same physical state within our bodies:</u> in both, the heart beats faster, and cortisol is released into the body to prepare it for action.*

Following this statement, a natural question comes up: If these physical reactions are the same, both in fear and excitement, then what makes the difference between the two?

The answer is simply *how our brain interprets a situation.*

When you are excited, the brain tells you that the experience you're about to have will be positive, and you will be looking forward to it. When you are afraid, your brain interprets a situation as negative and is looking to make you avoid it. What we are going to do is we are going to use the power of your mind to your advantage.

The standard advice you usually get when feeling anxious is most often something like "just try to calm down" or "feel the fear and do it anyway". But if you tried to calm down, you may have realized that it doesn't work. The reason is this: when you're feeling afraid, your body is in a high state of arousal, agitated, and your heart is racing; however, when you're calm, your body is relaxed, in a low arousal state.

That is why it's pretty much impossible to "just calm down". (Robbins, 2017)

So, what do you do when you have an exam, a presentation or have to talk to someone and you're afraid?

You say these three words to yourself: I AM EXCITED. If necessary, repeat them to yourself a couple of times.

Maybe some of you will think it is silly, and it won't work, but it's an effective way to trick your brain. It doesn't need to be complicated to be efficient.

> *You are telling your brain why your body is all agitated.*
> *Your mind will go from feeling agitation and making you afraid to reframing it into excitement.*

Such a small change makes such a big difference. In the studies that Harvard Business School made, researchers noticed that those who reappraised their anxiety as excitement gave better speeches and did better on tests. People were 17% more persuasive in their public lectures and had a 22% improvement when taking a test, compared to those who said nothing or tried to remain calm. (The Atlantic, 2016)

It's essential to note that the anxiety level stayed the same for everyone. All people remained in a high arousal state. Only the performance was significantly improved. It's incredible what just a simple change of perspective can do!

You might not be in control of how you feel, but you can always control what you think about.

The second thing I strongly suggest you do is visualizing a positive scenario. For instance, if you're nervous about holding a presentation in front of your colleagues, you most likely think that you will embarrass yourself in front of them. Instead of imagining this negative outcome, visualize yourself holding the presentation feeling confident, and perhaps that at the end of the lecture, your colleagues will be congratulating you for doing a great job.

So, always remember excitement and fear feel the same in your body. The only difference is how your brain calls it. You get yourself out of a threat mindset to an opportunity mindset by reframing your feelings and focusing on visualizing positive outcomes.

∼

Chapter 2: Key Takeaways

1. The idea that failure is bad has been ingrained in the collective mindset. However, we can change our perspective on it.

2. We tend to see things either black or white and believe there is either success or failure, but this type of thinking is to our detriment. In reality, every little step in the right way is important, and not every step towards growth will be a huge leap. Not only do small risks help one improve, but they lead to small failures. Regrouping after smaller mistakes is much easier than after the big ones.

3. Success can be compared to the image of an iceberg. Most people see what is on top of the surface but not what is "under the water". Beneath the surface is a lot of mistakes and failures that serve as a base for growth if we allow them.

4. One of the richest men in the world, Jeff Bezos, has had his fair share of failed businesses before having great success with Amazon. Even after starting Amazon, some mistakes were made with different product ideas. Still, they served only as stepping stones to success.

5. Cultivate a growth mindset: keep an open mind and continue to educate yourself, be perseverant when facing challenges, stay open to feedback and make sure you celebrate other people's successes.

6. You can trick your brain into replacing the feeling of fear with excitement. Fear and excitement result in the same physical state in our bodies. The difference between the two is how our brain interprets a situation —positive or negative. Instead of telling yourself that you feel so nervous and so scared to do something, you change it to telling yourself how excited you feel. Lastly, instead of thinking about all the possible negative outcomes, it is essential that you think about all the positive ones and visualize them.

GET OUT OF YOUR OWN HEAD

"The mind is a wonderful servant but a terrible master."

— ROBIN SHARMA

*P*icture your mind as a neglected garden. Weeds are taking over, and it's a chaotic mess. You wouldn't just plant new seeds and hope that something would grow. You would start by digging out the root of the weeds. If you try to chop them all off quickly, they will keep growing back. Though it takes more time and effort, digging deep and pulling them out by the root is the best way to clean things up.

Then, you'd plant your seeds and make sure they got water every day. It would take consistent nurturing.

Grow the garden that is your mind. Dig out the roots of the negative thoughts and plant fresh, healthy seeds. Check on it to ensure it is continually thriving.

The Habit of Overthinking

Fretting over a problem obsessively to the point that it is causing you stress and anxiety is what psychologists call rumination. It feels like a broken record that is stuck in your head, and the lyrics are all negative: it's replaying embarrassing situations, arguments you've had, and mistakes you've made.

We're all guilty of ruminating at one point or another in our lives. We want to believe that doing so will eventually get us the solutions we've been looking for. The more time you have to think, the higher the probability of finding the right answer, isn't it? Well, not really. Quite the opposite. Spinning the same thoughts over and over will just lead to stress and analysis paralysis. You will only keep dwelling on a problem. Even if you spend an hour or ten overthinking, it won't help you get to a conclusion.

Overthinking for hours makes you feel tired, and it becomes a destructive cycle because the more tired you are, the more likely you are to overthink and stress. It's a never-ending spiral.

The moment you become aware of these self-destructive behaviors, you're taking the first step towards change.

So, which types of behavior make you an overthinker? I will name a few of them:

- Rehashing your conversations with other people, thinking about all the things you wish you had or hadn't said.
- Second-guessing pretty much every decision you make.
- Having trouble sleeping because your brain refuses to shut off.
- Reliving embarrassing situations over and over in your head.
- Spending a significant amount of time thinking about what someone meant when they told you something.
- Regularly asking yourself "what if" questions.
- Often dwelling on things that happened in the past or worry about what could happen in the future.

It's essential when discussing this subject to know that _rumination is also normal and functional_. Concentrating your mind to fix a problem is positive; it only becomes an issue when it turns into a train of negative thoughts.

"Rumination is like an overgrown garden. There are weeds everywhere but flowers too, and it helps to know the difference"

— (AIKEN, 2017)

Thinking about specific situations is helpful, unlike generalizing when something bad happened. "What caused me to pass my deadline at work?" is better than asking yourself, "Why am I such a failure?". Think about realistic, defined goals and how to achieve them. Any thoughts that lead to decisions are beneficial.

The researcher Mario Mikulincer acknowledged the existence of three types of rumination:

1. *The state rumination* is when a person focuses on failure. For example, if someone spends hours or days wondering why they weren't successful at a job interview.

2. *The action rumination*: when a person thinks obsessively about what they can do to improve a situation – e.g., you had a fight with your partner, and now you lose your sleep thinking about how to make things better.

*3. **Task-irrelevant rumination*** is quite common: we ruminate about unrelated things, utilize events that are not associated with the blocked goal in order to distract us from a failure; an example could be choosing to binge-watch an entire season of a series so that you avoid thinking about a failed exam.

Excessive rumination had been associated with mental health issues like depression, anxiety, eating disorders, or addictions.

What can you do to stop rumination? Below I've shared a few action steps and cognitive-behavioral techniques you can apply when feeling stuck in your head and can't stop overthinking. You don't have to apply all of these, and most certainly not all at once. Depending on the situation you are confronting yourself with, you can use one strategy at a time or mix a few that you think will work best for you.

1. Take action: An overthinker will get stuck analyzing a problem. So, to fight this urge, focus on taking action. For example, if you're worried about an argument you had with a co-worker, rather than rehashing the situation, accept the fact you can't change what happened already. Focus instead on addressing the consequences: have a discussion with your co-worker, apologize or whatever might be needed and move on.

2. Challenge your thoughts. Overthinkers deal with negative self-talk, also known as cognitive distortions in psychology. When you're experiencing a cognitive distortion, the way you interpret events is usually negatively biased.

> "My boss asked me to see him in his office. Probably he is going to fire me."

"It's very late, and my sister didn't come home yet.
Something bad must have happened to her."

By interpreting a situation differently, you manage to make your negative thoughts less believable:

"My boss might just want to catch up on project updates."
"My sister probably stopped by the shop, and that's why she is running late."

This process is called cognitive restructuring – you reframe your thoughts, challenging the accuracy of the negative ones.

3. Refocus your attention: you should try to find an activity that will absorb you, so watching some TV probably won't hold your attention enough to stop the negative train of thoughts from your head. It's recommended to find a physical activity that will combine mental engagement and social contact: a walk in nature with a friend, calling someone, playing with your pet or kids, etc.

Keep in mind that any conversations should be steered away from the issue that's bugging you. If you choose to share with someone what's on your mind, make sure you're brainstorming for solutions rather than dissecting and revisiting negative aspects of the problem. Resist the urge to co-ruminate with your friend, as that would only increase your stress levels.

4. Slow down your thoughts: this is a method that works very well because when we are overthinking, our minds speed up to a point where our thoughts become barely recognizable. It is a cognitive technique that will change the way you relate to your thinking and how much control it has over you. Slowing down your internal dialogue will help decrease your anxiety; For example, if you're overwhelmed at work because you don't know how to do a particular task, the thought that comes up to your mind is, "Oh my God, I have no clue how to do this!". To practice the slowed-down inner dialogue, you'll have to say the phrase three times in your head, as if the words were playing at half-speed. After doing so, continue to slow down even more and say it two more times. Make sure you're breathing deeply. Notice how different you felt when you said the words first and how you feel saying them now. Your body feels so much more relaxed.

5. Micro-solutions: Often, when we're having these obsessive thoughts is because we feel overwhelmed. When we try to find a solution, but there are too many things to consider, we just end up feeling lost. We get lost in our thoughts instead of finding a solution and take action. A great way to do this is by asking yourself, "What is a small step that I could take now that will solve this problem? Once you have the answer, focus solely on it instead of being overwhelmed by the big picture.

6. Set a time-limit: If a problem requires your attention and you want to take some time to reflect on it, go ahead and worry about it, but set up a time-limit. For instance, twenty minutes per day should be enough. Put your timer on and worry as much as you want. Once the twenty minutes are up, you shouldn't spend another second on that matter. If you catch yourself worrying after that, remind yourself it is not the time, and if necessary, you can schedule twenty minutes the next day. This technique works better the more you practice it, and it will help you develop self-discipline. The people who tried this technique experienced significant improvements after only two weeks: their worries were reduced, their anxiety decreased, and they experienced better sleep.

The fact is that worrying knows no limits, so setting up a time constraint is necessary. Your mental wellness will improve, and you will be more productive. The time you were previously using to worry, you will now spend doing something more beneficial. Give yourself no more than twenty minutes a day. If another issue shows up and you will want to worry about it, schedule twenty minutes the next day.

7. Practice acceptance. Learning acceptance is essential when you are someone that is constantly overwhelmed with worry. The thing that makes you feel uneasy is something you're not willing to accept. It will likely start going away when you manage to make mental peace with it. The rule is this: if you can't change a situation, let it go.

The American theologian Reinhold Niebuhr wrote a beautiful serenity prayer that encompasses this idea very well: "God, grant me the serenity to accept the things I cannot change, the courage to change the things I can, and the wisdom to know the difference."

8. Cold showers: this method is efficient and straightforward. And I'll tell you why it works. A cold shower is an intense experience and takes you out of your mind and brings your awareness into your body. It is like forced meditation. It's difficult to overthink and worry when that cold water starts dripping down your back. Take few minutes and do a cold shower. It will slow down the train of thoughts present in your head, and even for a short while, will keep you away from ruminating.

9. Be patient: overthinking is a habit, and it will take a little bit of time until you will manage it better. So, there's no need to ruminate about the fact you can't stop ruminating.

Chapter 3: Key Takeaways

1. Rumination is defined as excessive, repetitive thinking about a situation. It is like a broken record that is stuck in your head, and the lyrics are all negative: it's replaying embarrassing situations, arguments you've had, and mistakes you've made.

2. It is essential to note that rumination to a certain degree is normal and functional. As long as you focus on fixing a problem, it's all good; it only becomes an issue when it turns into a train of negative thoughts.

3. Excessive rumination leads to high levels of stress and has been associated with mental health issues like depression, anxiety, eating disorders, or addictions.

How can you stop rumination?

- Push yourself to take action regarding the matter that is worrying you.
- Reframe your negative thoughts. By interpreting a situation differently, you will manage to make your negative thoughts less believable.
- Refocus your attention on an activity that will absorb you.
- Slow down your thoughts.
- Focus on micro-solutions.
- Set a time-limit for your worries.
- Practice acceptance.

- Take a cold shower to bring your focus to the body and stop ruminating.
- Be patient. Stopping the habit of overthinking will not happen in few days, so allow yourself time to change this self-destructing behavior.

DO IT IMPERFECTLY

"And now that you don't have to be perfect, you can be good."

— JOHN STEINBECK, EAST OF EDEN

What is one thing you could describe as perfect? Is it the pizza you ordered last night? Your favorite movie? A really nice outfit you bought for yourself?

Perfect is a blanket term to describe different scenarios. You can have a perfect date. You can mix cocktails perfectly. Your spouse might be perfect for you. Though it can be used to describe many different scenarios, it's much harder to actually find.

Those who become obsessed with the idea of perfection can get lost in their desire to achieve it. Chasing perfection is flawed because we overlook the greatness in the things that we already have accomplished.

The healthy kind of perfectionism is a driving force, motivating you to push through and achieve your goals. But when it goes out of control, it becomes a path to stress and unhappiness.

Positive or adaptive perfectionists enjoy challenges and work hard for their success, with their mindset oriented towards achievement; maladaptive perfectionists, on the other hand, have a negative focal point, concentrating more on avoiding failure. They tend to have a rigid all-or-nothing type of thinking, a tendency to avoid challenges, to procrastinate, and to make unhealthy comparisons. Driven by the fear of failure, low self-esteem, and adverse experiences during childhood, extreme perfectionism is often associated with compulsive behaviors, depression, anxiety, eating disorders, or suicidal impulses. It can also make some feel unworthy of love and belonging, resulting in perceived social isolation.

Even if perfectionists are more motivated and conscientious, the crippling anxiety outweighs any of those benefits (Breidenthal, Bujold, Harari, & Swider, 2018).

The most common signs of maladaptive perfectionism include:

- Setting unrealistically high expectations for oneself and others.
- Very critical of mistakes and very quick to find flaws.
- Strong tendency to procrastinate due to fear of failure.
- Looking for approval and validation from certain people.
- A tendency to shrug off and minimize compliments or successes.

Noticing flaws is not always a bad thing. It is a survival instinct. However, like most mental armor, we need to make sure we manage how it affects our thoughts; otherwise, it becomes destructive. We must learn to accept the flaws of the world and in ourselves. Trying to achieve perfection can rob you of appreciation for the things that are already pretty great around you. It can keep you stuck because it's an impossible state to achieve.

Generational Differences

A study by Thomas Curran and Andrew Hill examining generational differences regarding perfectionism shows over the past 30 years, people's desire (especially youngsters) to be flawless has skyrocketed!

The study, which was also published in the journal Psychological Bulletin, analyzed data from 41,000 college students from the United States, Canada, and the United Kingdom.

They studied generational changes in perfectionism from the late 1980s to 2016. During their analysis, Curran and Hill investigated three types of perfectionism:

1. Self-oriented perfectionism: demanding perfection from oneself.
2. Other-oriented perfectionism: having unrealistic standards of perfection from others.
3. Socially prescribed perfectionism: perceiving excessive expectations of perfection from others.

According to statistics, between 1989 and 2016, the socially prescribed perfectionism increased by an incredible 33%, self-oriented perfectionism increased by 10%, while other-oriented perfectionism increased by 16%. (Curran, T., & Hill, A. P, 2019)

One very important aspect mentioned by the authors of the study is that this increase in perfectionism is accompanied by psychological difficulties. Global health estimates made by the World Health Organization in 2017 show that various mental health conditions like body dysmorphia, eating disorders, depression, and anxiety affect a record number of young people.

Even though more research is necessary to confirm this, it has been speculated that one of the factors that profoundly influenced this rise in perfectionism is social media, which adds pressure by creating an environment where we continuously compare to others.

The researchers also think that millennials are now experiencing increasingly unrealistic educational and professional expectations. During the mid-70s, only half of the high-school seniors were expected to get a college degree. That number increased by a staggering 80% by 2008.

The Compassionate Self-talk: An antidote for perfectionism's side effects

An Australian study made recently shows that self-compassion balances out depression caused by maladaptive perfectionism. To get a visual representation of it, have a look at the diagram below:

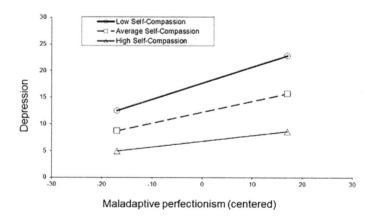

source: www.ncbi.nlm.nih.gov

This study was made on a group of 541 adolescents and 515 adults who anonymously filled in questionnaires designed to assess the correlation between self-compassion, perfectionism, and depression. This research concluded that those experiencing high levels of maladaptive perfectionism are less prone to develop depressive symptoms within the context of high self-compassion.

It is important to be noted that there is a difference between self-compassion and not pushing yourself to do better or not having any ambition. Too much self-compassion and cutting yourself slack can undermine your ability to cope with adversity and resilience. Playing it safe and not taking risks will cause you to stagnate. Keep pushing your limits while setting realistic and challenging goals.

I've been a perfectionist my entire life, so learning self-compassion has proved to be more difficult than I expected. It's crazy how we find it so easy to be nice and understanding to others but have a hard time doing that with ourselves. But I'm working on it. We're all work in progress in one aspect or another, and I'm no exception.

My habit of comparing myself to others created so much internal suffering and made a mark on my self-confidence. *"Comparison is the thief of joy",* as Theodore Roosevelt said.

If you don't learn to put a stop to it, it ends up making you feel miserable. I've wasted so much time comparing my looks, bank account, social skills, sense of humor to others. And guess what? There was always someone else who was smarter, prettier, funnier, and more successful. There's no win in this sort of competition. We just fill ourselves with resentment towards ourselves and others when participating in this toxic game.

Time is precious. Spending even one second of our lives comparing to another person is too much time. We all have a unique journey, different lessons to learn, and different purposes. Any type of comparison is unfair, like comparing apples to pears and butterflies to elephants. Focus on your own failures, successes, and growth.

Think about when you're driving — if you get distracted by looking at the car next to you for very long, you lose focus from the road and will probably get yourself into an accident. That's how life works as well. Looking too much at others' beauty or accomplishments makes you lose focus and not truly value your own.

Society's definition of success focuses too much on external achievements and forgets to pay attention to internal success – your inner peace, confidence, level of connection with others, or love. While some might have financial success, they could lack health. While some might have a great career, they could lack inner peace. I don't want to diminish the importance of achievements in life. Both external and internal success contribute to a feeling of fulfillment, but external success will always feel empty without the internal one. You are not in competition with anyone else but yourself. Especially now, in the age of social media, it's not easy to stay away from unhealthy comparisons. I love social media, but from this point of view, it really doesn't make things any easier for us. For example, I use Instagram, and I've unfollowed all the glamorous, super-duper cool people there. I've only kept connections with friends or business-related. I did it because the toxic comparisons are inevitable and made me feel bad about myself, distracting me from my journey and the blessings I already have.

I heard a saying not long time ago, and it stuck with me:

"There can only be one Beatles, but that doesn't mean other people shouldn't make music."

Think about it for a second. Taking this music-related example specifically — there have been written hundreds of thousands of songs over time. Some better than others. But what is important is that the next artist didn't say to himself: "Aw, you know what, there are already a lot of great songs out there, mine probably won't even be that good, so what's the point?" No! That artist just made a new song from the bottom of his heart, shared it with the world, and hoped people would enjoy it.

As long as you are putting in your best effort, that is enough! You are enough!

When you actually realize that doing the best you can is sufficient, even if it's not perfect, you will understand there is room for everybody. You are you, and nobody else can be the same. Understand that this is your power. You should only compare yourself with the person you were yesterday and no one else.

"A flower does not think of competing to the flower next to it. It just blooms."

— ZEN SHIN

Wabi-Sabi — A Japanese Philosophy

Have you ever heard about wabi-sabi? If not, well, wabi-sabi is a Japanese concept that focuses on accepting flaws and seeing the beauty in imperfection.

"Wabi" is defined as "rustic simplicity" or "understated elegance", focusing on a less-is-more mentality.
"Sabi" means "taking pleasure in the imperfect."
(Japanahome, 2020)

If the chase for perfection in all the aspects of our lives often leads to stress, anxiety, and depression, wabi-sabi invites for a pause. It encourages us to be grateful and count our blessings, *celebrating the way things are and not how they should be.*

Wabi-sabi's timeless wisdom is more relevant now than ever for modern life, as we search for meaning and fulfillment beyond materialism. It values the beauty of imperfection, tranquility, and harmony. It encompasses the appreciation for the things we have, the people we love, finding enjoyment and gratitude in everything we do.

The art of kintsugi is an excellent example of wabi-sabi, where cracked pottery is filled with gold-dusted lacquer in order to showcase the beauty of its age and damage rather than hiding it. The fault is highlighted, not hidden.

Robyn Griggs Lawrence, the author of "Simply Imperfect: Revisiting the Wabi-Sabi House" says:

"Bringing wabi-sabi into your life doesn't require money, training, or special skills. It takes a mind quiet enough to appreciate muted beauty, courage not to fear bareness, willingness to accept things as they are — without ornamentation. It depends on the ability to slow down, to shift the balance from doing to being, to appreciating rather than perfecting."

Becoming an Action Taker

"Action may not always bring happiness, but there is no happiness without action."

— BENJAMIN DISRAELI, FORMER
BRITISH PRIME MINISTER

To do, or not to do, that is the question!

We get petrified in the face of uncertainty. We prefer the safety of our comfort zones instead of gathering some courage and changing something that's bothering us. Oh, that miserable, safe comfort!

All of us stayed at some point in an unfulfilling job, unhappy relationship, or other negative environments because we were too scared to change something. What's outside of our little world makes us afraid because it is unfamiliar. And that's ok. Fear is normal. But you know what? Nobody is going to come to rescue you.

You need to be your own hero. Until you don't make a change, nothing changes.

When I was still an employee, I used to hope every day that some miracle will happen, and I won't have to go and work at my job. I won't need to see another day of misery. But nothing changed until I decided enough is enough and took matters into my own hands. You might not be able to quit your job tomorrow or leave a negative situation you find yourself in right away but start thinking about your exit strategy as soon as possible. Just "hoping" is not going to take you anywhere. Hiding under a blanket and believing the monsters of real-life won't find you is immature and ineffective.

I love this quote by Yvon Chouinard, which sums up beautifully my point: "There's no difference between a pessimist who says, 'Oh, it's hopeless, so don't bother doing anything,' and an optimist who says, 'Don't bother doing anything, it's going to turn out fine anyway.' Either way, nothing happens."

Fear has many faces and can hide even under the mask of hope and optimism.

Nike, the well-known sportswear brand, has my favorite slogan: Just do it! It calls for action. Without action, it's impossible to create anything. What I would add to the slogan in this context is the word "badly". Just do it badly!

Lowering your ideals of perfection is a simple way to push yourself to take action and avoid procrastination.

It is a great mental strategy. Simple methods like this can often make the difference between preserving your mental health, living a quality life, and suffering a great negative mental impact, dealing with anxiety-related disorders.

It's time to stop wasting hours trying to decide what to do. Just get it done. If it turns out the way you wanted it — that's wonderful! If not, you will learn something in the process that will help you grow. Forget about perfection. Seek progress. This means learning something valuable every day. Things happen naturally, unexpectedly, and imperfectly.

We can't force how we learn. Perfection isn't a state where we can live in accordance with the natural flow of events. Do the best you can at all times and find peace in knowing that you gave your best shot.

Also, don't be resistant. Don't try to force change—especially when dealing with other people. Your family, friends, your career, and the Universe all have different paces. Trying to force change is like trying to make a tree grow quicker. You can't do it! You just have to wait for it to happen on its own. Real, long-lasting, and meaningful change will take time, and the road to get there is less than perfect.

Starting something will always be the most challenging part. Get better at starting new things: Do you have a book to write? Open up your computer. Do you want to lose weight? Put on your gym shoes.

Starting is hard because we think of the entirety of the process, diving into all the potential scenarios, failures, and outcomes. Just start and take the first step. You might end up going in a different direction but putting that initial foot forward is enough to get your momentum going. The only way that you can truly get results is to do something in the first place. As Mark Twain once said, "The secret to getting ahead is getting started."

Putting effort into something makes the end results so much better. Recently, I had a big, exhausting move. I hadn't uprooted in a while, so the house was certainly chaotic. As I moved into the new place and started to unpack, I found myself growing angry. I was stressed that I had so many clothes to organize, I was dreading having to put up all the artwork and decide where to place my plants. Then it hit me. Why was I mad? I had been trained to think of these tasks as exhausting labor. In reality, it was thrilling! I was starting a completely new adventure. I wasn't just setting things up the way they were at my last home. I was creating a new environment where I could fully express myself.

It was a struggle to lift heavy boxes up and down the stairs, and anyone who has moved knows the frustration of missing the one box you need something from! However, even though this struggle was messy, exhausting, and imperfect, it was a journey I took to achieve a personal goal. Now, when I sit down on my cozy couch in my beautiful home, I feel so proud. I look at all the work I put into making this my place, and I feel at peace. I wouldn't have done it any other way. If someone else had done all the work for me, maybe I wouldn't be able to fully love and appreciate my home in the way I do now.

Start right where you are and pick-up whatever tools you have. As you continue on your journey, you will build resistance and strength. The longer you wait to start, the further away from enjoying the end result you will be. It's easy to use up time tomorrow because it is not ours. The only thing that is ours is the time we have in the present moment.

Procrastination

Perfectionism and procrastination come hand in hand. Perfectionists have real trouble getting things done, mostly because of their high, unachievable standards. They fear failure, which eventually leads to avoidance behaviors.

Procrastination is not the same as laziness. A lazy person is apathetic and inactive, while a procrastinator chooses to postpone certain tasks in favor of more pleasant activities. Procrastination is a temporary relief from something that's stressing us out. We postpone those tasks that seem tedious or daunting and choose to do more enjoyable things, like surfing the web, binge-watching TV series, or hanging out with friends.

Alternatively, you might be a productive procrastinator if you fill your time with low-priority tasks. This type of procrastination allows you to temporarily ignore what you should be doing while still being productive. It provides fulfillment that alleviates some of the guilt brought on by skipping the task. For example, you might not feel guilty about skipping studying because you cleaned your entire apartment instead.

Procrastination just pushes back the pain that we will eventually have to deal with.

How to overcome procrastination and increase productivity?

1. Create a to-do list.

Boo! I know that you probably read about this over and over in the past, in which case it's not super exciting to read about it now but hear me out. This one is a classic tool, and even if most people know about it, they don't use it properly.

Your to-do list should be more than a desk decoration. I've had many days in the past when I've created a to-do list that just sat nicely on my desk for days as a beautiful ornament. I was the best at procrastinating. No one was ever able to beat me at it. I would sometimes tackle a little chore to feel productive while avoiding doing the important stuff.

The change for me was when I approached my to-do list differently and got more done in a week than the previous two months combined. No exaggeration!

First things first – make your to-do list the night before; don't waste time with it in the morning, as you'll lose momentum.

It's essential that you break down your tasks into the tiniest fragments possible so that you can quickly check things off and fly through tasks throughout the day. Instead of looking at your day and seeing one long, daunting battle, you'll see micro tasks that can be easily tackled. Biting off more than you can chew is the quickest way to make yourself feel frustrated and overwhelmed.

Most important is to start with realistic goals. Don't expect yourself to write a book in a day, especially if you've been putting off this project for years. It would be too much pressure trying to lose fifteen pounds in a month if you haven't worked out in years. Therefore, create a goal that you are excited about! If you look at the things you have to do with nothing but dread, you will only keep pushing them back.

Organize your to-do list according to your priorities. Choose only one task that will be your number one priority from the list; it should be the one thing that will bring you the highest return, that will have the most beneficial impact.

One of the best things you could do is adding a time frame for each task, so you know how much you will be able to fit in your calendar. A big mistake people make is they create a to-do list without being aware of the amount of time necessary to get things done. Make sure you will schedule everything, from checking your e-mails to calling friends, and most importantly, be aware of the breaks you'll need to take.

Checking your e-mail or messages sporadically throughout the day is eating more of your time than you realize; you might think it will only take you ten minutes, but you will probably still be there one hour later. So, schedule some time in the morning or late afternoon for it instead of getting distracted by all types of notifications throughout your entire day.

Fun fact: According to research, the average worker is only productive for 2 hours and 53minutes each 8 hours workday. (Ohio University, 2018)

You could be productive within an 8-hour workday, but only if breaks would be taken effectively, which very few people do.

Sweden introduced for a limited time the 6-hour workday and what they noticed was an increase in productivity and overall happiness of workers.

Working long hours with no breaks is a sure way to make yourself miserable and unproductive.

2. A useful tool for time management is the **Pomodoro technique**. It is a simple approach that involves chunking your time into 25-minute intervals. In between each 25-minute set, you will give yourself a 5-minute break. After two hours, you would then take a longer, 30-minute break. Doing this helps you to group your tasks together, so they don't feel that uncontrollable. Once you finish a 25-minute session, give yourself permission to use 5-minutes for whatever you want. You can sit and scroll on your phone. You can watch a funny video or eat a snack. Rather than telling yourself that you have to work for two hours before you get a break, this method makes things more manageable.

3. Use deadlines!

If you look at your schedule and tell yourself, "Hopefully, I can do this by next week", Good luck! However, I can tell you now that it won't work.

You need strict deadlines. I've had projects in the past that took me six months instead of one month, just because I wasn't specific enough regarding my deadline and didn't schedule for each day effectively.

4. Use Parkinson's law in your favor.

First, what is Parkinson's law? According to Parkinson's law, *work expands to fill the time available for its completion.* This means if you have a paper to work on by next week, it will be done by next week; if something must be done in 6 months, it will be done in 6 months. We always plan depending on how much time we have available, and when a deadline approaches, we start to actually take the necessary steps to complete the task by the deadline.

If you give yourself two weeks to complete a three-hour task, the task will appear more complex from a psychological perspective and will fill those two weeks scheduled for completion. If you assign the right amount of time to a task, then you gain back more time, as you will try your best to finish by the given deadline.

Now, it doesn't mean you have to set unrealistic deadlines. You can't write a book in a day or build a house in a week. You need to be reasonable about how much time you will need for a task and cut that buffer time that most of us add when scheduling certain tasks.

I think you can best use Parkinson's law if you ask yourself: "What would it look like if I worked on my project on a very aggressive timescale?" This type of question will allow you to brainstorm and discover different approaches you can use to get the work done in less time.

Most people have an inflated idea of how long a task takes to complete. You will only become aware of how quickly some tasks get completed when you test this principle.

Go and make your to-do list and divide it by the amount of time it takes to complete each assignment. After that, give yourself half of that time to complete the tasks. The time limit has to be seen as crucial. If you will think, "Oh, it's not a big deal that I passed the due date", this won't work. See these deadlines you set for yourself as unbreakable.

Like Elon Musk once said:

"Stop being patient and start asking yourself: How do I accomplish my ten-year plan in six months? You will probably fail, but you will be a lot further along than the person who simply accepted that it was going to take ten years!"

---

5. The biggest enemy of productivity is lack of focus, so choose a space where you can work in silence, with the least amount of things that can distract you and turn off notifications on your phone or laptop.

Don't wait to feel motivated

There is a big misconception around the fact that we have to feel motivated in order to get things done. But motivation is a capricious thing! Sometimes you feel motivated, but after only a few days, the feeling is gone. Sometimes you wait for it, but it just doesn't turn up. It's not there when you need it! So, you can't rely your productivity and life on it.

If you've been operating from this "motivation before action" mentality – sorry to tell you, but you've had it backwards this whole time! But I get it. I used to do the same. I waited to feel motivated to get up early, go to the gym, or work on my business. Sometimes you might be able to get motivated for a short while, but once motivation starts to fade, you will stop taking action.

That is why when people start going to the gym, they are super excited for the first three days, and then it gets more and more difficult for them to go out and do it. They wait to be motivated!

Instead, small actions need to be taken, and motivation will follow.

It all starts with action!

Most people think motivation works in this order: motivation – action – more motivation, when in reality it works like this: action – motivation – more motivation. (Bokhari, n.d)

Action leads to motivation, not the other way around!

If you hesitate to take action, most times is because you feel overwhelmed by the magnitude of a project, the amount of time, work, and effort it will take.

So, as suggested in the previous section, when we discussed overcoming procrastination, the key to getting started is to make whatever you need to do, look approachable.

Deep cleaning your entire house today might seem too much, and you wouldn't feel like doing it. Only thinking about how much time and effort it would require will make you want to go and watch some Netflix. However, that is just postponing something that you will need to do either way. Just scheduling to do a small part of that in one day will be a more realistic and approachable goal. Divide your big tasks into smaller ones and then take a small action in order to build some momentum.

If you want to feel motivated to go for a workout, choose a single simple step you can do, like putting your training shoes on. If you want to feel motivated to do some work, go to your desk and open your laptop.

If you want to start waking up earlier, let's say at 5.30 a.m., but you wake up usually at 8.00 a.m., then set your alarm fifteen minutes earlier than your regular wake-up time for a week. Once you get used to the new waking time, again set the alarm fifteen minutes earlier and keep doing so until you get to the desired wake-up time.

This process is literally for anything you want to accomplish in your life:

1. Think about something you wanted to do for a while but haven't felt motivated to start. Write it down on a piece of paper if you wish.
2. Take a simple action step right at that moment in order to make some progress with your goal.

If you need a push even for this small first step, then read on...

3, 2, 1, Go!

I know that sometimes you don't feel like you want to take even the smallest step. No matter if the reason is your lack of motivation, that you're scared or nervous, the "3,2,1, Go!" method is here to push you and make you an action taker. What do you have to do? Just don't give yourself too much time to think. You have to count down, from three to one and then go take action. If you start to think about it, your brain will eventually convince you not to do it. I usually use this method when my fears are trying to keep me from getting out of my comfort zone.

Our minds are looking to protect us from what is scary or uncomfortable, and this is why you have to move faster than your brain! You know there is nothing dangerous about working out or writing an e-mail. Some things might feel scary, but they are not literally dangerous. Your brain has the best intention to protect you but just ends up sabotaging you. Let's say you are at a party and want to start a conversation with someone but feel nervous. Pondering too much about it will make you feel so anxious that, in the end, it will make you change your mind.

So just count to yourself 3-2-1 and GO!

The counting itself will distract you from the excuses, anxiety, or other thoughts you might be having in your mind. If you didn't press the "Go" button when you said you would, then you won't be doing it anymore. The countdown is meant to help you move. Each step you will take will bring you a little bit closer to your goal, no matter if that is having great fitness, starting your business, changing your job, or meeting someone new.

Everybody wants to be healthy, financially free, happy, and have great relationships, but only very few people actually wake up and do the doing.

You will still have to push yourself! Having just three seconds available will outsmart your brain. However, it is not a magic formula — you will have to want it bad enough.

Even if it's something so simple, it will make you feel very uncomfortable in the beginning. It won't be necessarily easy, but practicing will make it better in time. Each small effort will add up, and a year from now, you will be amazed at your accomplishments.

Waiting around is just a way to look for more excuses. By pushing something back, we get the chance to ignore that anxiety over having to complete a task. We will push it back because we don't feel ready, don't have the knowledge, mood, etc. There will always be another reason we could wait. Our minds are very creative when it comes to finding excuses.

Do you know someone in your life who likes to talk about what they are going to do? They might go on and on about all the businesses they will start and the many ideas they have but never actually follow through with any of those. Maybe you are this type of person, which is perfectly fine. Having creative ideas is wonderful; however, they are worthless if you don't really put them into action. There will never be a right time to get things done. We could wait forever, but there will never be a moment that feels perfect.

"When it feels scary to jump, that's exactly when you jump. Otherwise, you end up staying in the same place your whole life."

— J.C. CHANDOR

Chapter 4: Key Takeaways

1. Perfectionism can be a driving force or a factor of stress, depending on whether we let it influence us in a positive way or allow it to go out of control and affect us negatively. An excessive focus on being perfect can keep us stuck in life, making us afraid to take action on our personal goals.

2. According to research, millennials feel a stronger pressure from society to be perfect compared to the previous generations. Things like social media had a saying in this aspect, making people feel more insecure due to the fact they continuously compare to others.

3. Maladaptive perfectionism has been linked to mental issues like depression, anxiety, or eating disorders.

4. It's been proved by research that treating ourselves with more compassion and being more accepting of our flaws has a beneficial impact on our mental wellbeing, making us less likely to experience anxiety or depression.

5. The Japanese concept of wabi-sabi invites us to be more accepting and find beauty in imperfection. The art of kintsugi is a great example of wabi-sabi, where cracked pottery is filled with gold lacquer.

6. Allowing ourselves to make mistakes can be a freeing experience. Instead of trying to make something perfect, we should concentrate on taking the first step, no matter how imperfect and flawed that might be. It is a good practice that will eventually help us become better action takers.

7. Procrastination is a by-product of perfectionism. We procrastinate in order to avoid daunting, monotonous tasks and also to prevent a potential failure. There are simple tools we can use, like the to-do lists, Pomodoro technique, or Parkinson's law, which help us greatly to overcome procrastination and increase our productivity.

8. Most people fail to achieve their life goals because they lack proper motivation. Most people were misled by the idea that they would need to feel motivated in order to progress with a personal goal, task, or project. However, this is not true. The truth is that action leads to motivation and not the other way around. Choosing a simple step that you could take right away is the secret to building up motivation.

9. There will never be a perfect time to get things done. Our brains' goal is to keep us safe and comfortable, which is why we need to find ways to go around our critical thinking, like the "3,2,1 go" strategy, so it doesn't stop us from taking action.

THE 3 SECRET INGREDIENTS FOR ACHIEVEMENT

*I*ngredient #1: Courage

"Courage doesn't always roar. Sometimes courage is the quiet voice at the end of the day saying: I will try again tomorrow"

— MARY ANNE RADMACHER

As I was saying in the introduction, our attitude towards failure is what holds the utmost importance when it comes to our level of achievement in life. But digging deeper, I noticed that the fear of failure is not the problem itself but rather a consequence of a bigger issue: self-doubt.

We have trouble believing in ourselves, so we miss our goals. We doubt the internal power and skills we have. We fear taking risks. We accept less than we deserve. This is why we stay in toxic relationships and in jobs we hate.

The irony of life is that smart people are the ones most affected by self-doubt. They think about every possible obstacle they could encounter. And this ability to anticipate any potential problem or negative outcome keeps them stuck in their heads, not allowing them to take action.

Look around, and you will see that those people who dare to grab the bull by the horns are the ones that win at the game of life. They are not the most intelligent or knowledgeable. Courage/boldness/self-confidence — whatever you want to call it — is a better indicator of success than intelligence. Smart people think about all the possible negative outcomes, while the bold ones are looking for ways to figure things out. It doesn't mean smart people cannot be bold and vice versa, but only that most often, courage is the missing piece from the puzzle of success.

A lot of people make less money than they could've because they don't dare to ask. A survey was made not long ago, which included over 100,000 people who believed they were getting paid less than their actual value. Interestingly, even though these people thought they deserved to make more, two-thirds of people never asked for a raise.

Do you know what's even more interesting? From the one-third that asked for a raise, 70% got one. Therefore, you need to be bold enough to ask for what you want!

I used to work at this company a while ago, and according to my contract, after a year, I was supposed to have a review. Everybody is looking forward to the yearly evaluation because that's when their wage will supposedly be increased. But weeks went by, and there was no sign of it. Also, I felt that there was never the right moment to ask about it. I even made up excuses for my superiors, thinking that maybe they were too busy with their work. I kept hoping they were planning to do it, and I won't have to be the one asking for it. But one year and six months later, I was on the same (pathetic) salary.

During all this time, I wanted to say something, but my noisy brain didn't allow me to do so: "What if they're going to tell me that I'm doing a poor job? What if they will fire me? What if..."

After spending months struggling with these nagging thoughts, I decided to e-mail my boss. I told him that I want to have a performance appraisal. We scheduled it a few days later, and guess what? I was neither fired nor was told that I was bad at my job. The other way around actually – they were pleased with my work, and my salary got increased. Yay!! Six months later, though! Six months during which I could have been paid a higher wage. But I kept delaying it because I couldn't gather the courage to ask. On the bright side, I did learn a valuable lesson: if you don't go for what you want and if you don't ask for it, then there is zero chance for you to achieve it. As Wayne Gretzky said, "You miss 100% of the shots you don't take."

One of the worst things you can do is to self-reject. I know so many people that didn't go for what they wanted because they didn't believe in themselves. They didn't think they were smart enough, prepared enough, or good-looking enough. And I was one of those too, for so long.

When I was in college, I had the opportunity to be a part of an Erasmus project, which meant I had the chance to go for a semester to study abroad. The possibilities I had at the time were to go to Spain or Germany. Spain would have been my number one choice, but I thought my language skills weren't that great, and I would end up failing the language test I was supposed to take. So, I excluded that option and went with my second one – Germany. I passed the language test, and the second step of the application process was to attend an interview. But you know what I did? I didn't go because I thought that probably I don't have a real chance and I'm just wasting my time.

Do you know what the most painful part of this was? When another girl from my University applied for Spain, she barely passed the language test (by the way, I'm confident that my Spanish skills were better than hers) and ended up going for a semester there. Later, she told me it was the best experience of her entire life! I wanted to punch myself in the face when I heard that!! It could have been me, but I chose to self-reject.

So, amigos mios, please chase your dreams and goals. Even if you think you might not be the ideal candidate for a job, send your application. Even if you think someone will say "no" when you ask them out for a date, try your luck. It's better to try and fail than not take any chance and wonder for the rest of your life what could have happened. Take risks and don't accept anything less than you deserve. Be stubborn when it comes to achieving your objectives. Don't take the first "no" you hear. Have faith in your own capabilities!

Keep in mind that confidence is not something you're born with. It's something you build throughout your life. Some people will indeed be more confident than others at the beginning of their lives (depending on genetics and other circumstances), but it doesn't mean that you can't have it if you are not born with it. It's a skill, and like any other skill, it can be developed!

The Rejection Challenge

"There is only one way to avoid criticism: do nothing, say nothing, and be nothing."

— ARISTOTLE

The author and entrepreneur Jia Jiang realized a few years ago that his fear of rejection was holding him back in many aspects of his life. He didn't want to continue his existence like that, so he decided to do something about it. In 2012, he came across a game called "Rejection Therapy" that challenged people to seek rejection in their day-to-day lives. Jia committed to 100 days of rejection – he would purposely go out there and get rejected by asking all sort of favors from strangers, some more outrageous than the others: from asking a hotel to let him sleep for free in one of their rooms to requesting a "burger refill" at a restaurant or asking to borrow 100$ from a stranger. He was taken by surprise when some people accommodated his requests, like Krispy Kreme that agreed to link few donuts in the shape of the Olympic symbol for him.

On his first attempt, he was timid, and the moment he heard "no" from the other person, he just wanted to run away. But with each day of the challenge, he grew a thicker skin and realized that getting rejected wasn't that bad. He learned that the world was scarier in his head; Jiang said that most often, people proved to be open and eager to help.

He noticed that on many occasions, he was able to turn a "no" into a "yes" if he took the time to put himself in the other person's shoes. By asking a simple "why not?" he gave people the opportunity to share why they weren't comfortable accepting his request. With empathy and persistence, sometimes a "no" can be turned around.

He wrote in his book:

"My goal is to turn rejection into opportunity. I always thought it was something to run away from, but if we can embrace it, we can turn it into a lot more than an obstacle." He continued, saying: *"When you are not afraid of rejection, and it feels like you have nothing to lose, amazing things can happen."*

The more we get rejected, the less painful it becomes!

Rejection most often is not personal, even if it might feel like it is. It has more to do with the person who rejects you (their mood or circumstances) than it has to do with you.

There are many opportunities we miss because we are so afraid even to ask a question.

Challenging yourself to go out there will thicken your skin, and you should use rejection as fuel to be more determined. Most often, success is a numbers game, and you just have to swim through rejections until you get a "yes".

The most successful people have encountered rejection and obstacles but didn't allow them to define their lives:

- Walt Disney was fired from one of his jobs for not being creative enough.
- J.K Rowling had the Harry Potter series rejected twelve times before managing to publish it.
- Colonel Sanders had his chicken recipe rejected over 1,000 times before he was able to start KFC.
- Steve Jobs was fired from his own company, which only motivated him more. He eventually was able to return to Apple.
- Oprah Winfrey was told she is not made for television.
- Tesla, Elon Musk's company, almost failed before becoming the success that is today.

And this list could continue for many pages, but I think these few examples are enough to prove my point.

As Van Gogh famously said:

"If you hear a voice within you say, 'you cannot paint', then by all means paint, and that voice will be silenced."

Ready for a Challenge?

The most effective way to overcome the fear of rejection is to face it. And this being said, I have a challenge for you: in the upcoming 90 days, push yourself to go through rejection ten times.

My suggestion would be to start with small things, like asking a stranger for a dollar. Then, when you get more comfortable, you can go to the next level and ask for a pay rise at your job. You could have fun with this challenge and go ask a celebrity for a date or an interview.

Another option would be to focus on achieving one important personal goal. Write down a big objective you have and then make ten attempts at it within the next 90 days. Make a journal and write about your progress.

The options are endless, use your imagination and don't let your brain convince you something is off-limits.

With each challenge and rejection, you will become more resilient. You'll realize that fear is so much worse in your head than in reality. A lot of people quit after they tried something once. Even more people don't even take that first attempt towards a goal because they're not confident enough, and they self-reject (like yours truly has done in the past). Taking on this challenge can help you make progress on some big goals. It will desensitize you from the fear of failure and rejection. Don't focus so much on success. The idea is to grow a thicker skin and see that the world is not so bad as it may seem sometimes. Playing it safe is no way to live. Don't let the fear of rejection hold you back from so many potentially great opportunities. Go out there and do something bold!

As Norman Vincent Peale said:

"Shoot for the moon. Even if you miss, you'll land among the stars."

The ones who dare and don't see quitting as an option end up achieving success.

Ingredient #2: The people around you

"Show me your friends, and I'll tell you who you are" is an old and wise proverb. The people you surround yourself with will have one of the biggest impacts on your life and the level of success you will achieve.

American author and entrepreneur Jim Rohn thinks we are the average of the five people we spend the most time with. Besides our circle of friends, outside influences play a major part. Even celebrities or those who we follow on social media can significantly impact our life and behavior.

The rule is simple: if you want positivity in your life, you shouldn't hang around with people that drag your spirit down. Some people always find a reason why something can't be done, and if we continue to be surrounded by them, it will reflect in our reality. Toxic people sometimes stick around for far too long. Even though you've had certain friends for a long time, it doesn't mean you need to keep them around if they negatively influence you. It's all right to let go of old relationships. Friendships we started ten years ago might not be relevant for our present lives.

There is undoubtedly a strong pressure from our society to be social. Networking is encouraged, and the truth is, it's always nice to have a large group of friends. However, we might end up giving too much of our time to people who are undeserving of it.

To flourish, one should get involved in that community for which they want to find improvement. Hence, if you are trying to lose weight, you can find communities through your gym. If you're going to start or grow a business, you might want to find a team of entrepreneurs or even a mentor to help guide you in your business endeavors. It is crucial that we focus on surrounding ourselves with people who help us thrive. It is one of the most important things that will prepare us for success. (Sugar Hill, 2020)

Same way, misery loves company, so does success. Make sure you surround yourself with winners, people that can help you and inspire you to grow. Even if you don't have successful friends to surround yourself with, that's ok. In the era of technology, you don't have to limit yourself to those people nearby you. There is the magic of the internet, and you can reach pretty much anyone; search for mentors that have the success, health, wealth, or whatever else you desire and learn from them. Join groups with like-minded people. Look up to your idols and study them. Where did they start? What failures did they overcome? What setbacks were presented to them? Where are they now? Listen to interviews, read their books, and get a sense of how their minds work. The more you learn from them, the more you become like them.

If you don't want to be mediocre, stop hanging around mediocre people.

Pay close attention to your close friends and how they inspire you. If you could thank them for teaching you something, what would that be? Pick your people carefully, and actively assess the way they affect your life. The five closest people are a reflection of you since you chose them.

And now, as an exercise, I want you to put this book down and take a minute to think and choose an important objective you have and take a first step towards joining a group of people that have the same goal. Do a google search, go through Facebook groups, think about someone you would like to have as a mentor.

Please don't go to the next section of this book until you've done so. Remember, you are here to make little by little positive changes and become an action taker, not just acquire some information you don't plan to use.

Ingredient #3: Self-discipline

The economist James Heckman asked a number of people how big of a role they think innate intelligence has in financial success. The question was, "How much of a difference do you think there is, financially speaking, between person A and person B based on their IQ?"

Most people guessed somewhere around 25%, while others went higher, around 50%. However, Heckman's research concluded something completely different: innate intelligence plays at best between 1% and 2% in someone's future success. He said that success is correlated with self-discipline and consistency, more than it has to do with brains. (Flam, 2016)

Anything worth having takes time...

Mastering a skill, building a strong relationship with a partner, building your dream career or business requires dedication. Everything that is worth having needs some time investment on your side. As Bryant McGill said,

---

"Everything worthwhile takes time, nurturing, and love. When something isn't working, love it more, nurture it more and give it more time."

This is a big lesson for everyone, myself included. On the bright side, I'm an ambitious individual, but the downside is that I want everything yesterday. I'm one of the most impatient people out there. Learning patience and discipline have definitely been some of my biggest life lessons.

Short-term thinking is specific to poor people. They want to get fast results, craving that instant gratification. Prosperous people know the importance of sustained effort, consistent work, and the need to sacrifice today for a better tomorrow. Poor people would rather have a better today, preferring to watch TV, spending all their time relaxing. But this always comes at the cost of tomorrow. Short-term thinking is why most people don't achieve anything great.

How do you know if this short-term thinking characterizes you and your daily actions? Well, if you choose to spend time in front of the TV, playing video games, eating fast food often, sleeping-in, spending your money on items that don't do anything for your future (clothes, gadgets) instead of waking up to do something productive, eating healthy and investing in your future makes you a short-term thinker.

All these small decisions on what you do with your time today, what you eat today, how you spend your money today will add up and have consequences. Not doing the right thing will leave you broke, unhealthy and miserable.

Sure, you're only human, so allow yourself to indulge in the pleasures of life but have discipline. You could have a strict schedule and diet during the week and allow yourself to sleep in and relax during the weekends.

Improving self-discipline and motivation

In the previous chapter, I mentioned how important it is not to rely solely on motivation to do things, as motivation is short-lived. It is crucial to cultivate self-discipline. So, let's get deeper into discussing how motivation works and how you can improve it through discipline.

After you start, full of excitement, a new project, a new diet, or building a new habit, your motivation begins declining after a while. Only a few weeks or days later, you don't feel like continuing. Why does this happen?

Well, your brain is wired to protect you, so it will always try to make you avoid difficult and uncomfortable activities. Therefore, you will always prefer watching TV or scrolling through social media instead of working on your business, exercising, studying, or other productive tasks that, in the long term, would bring you greater benefits.

But maybe you noticed that some people seem to have this ability to consistently work towards their goals, even if it's inconvenient. This brings in the question: How are they any different? To find out what sets apart the people who manage to get a lot done, staying consistently productive, from those who can't help themselves from overly indulging in the simple pleasures of life, looking for short-term benefits, we need to talk about a brain neurotransmitter called dopamine.

Dopamine plays a vital role in the science of motivation. It is also known as the feel-good neurotransmitter: it is released when we consume comfort food, when we watch TV, when we listen to music – basically anything that makes us feel good. Dopamine has an extremely powerful influence on our behavior.

Few neuroscientists did some interesting research on the influence of dopamine in rats. At the beginning of the experiment, they have implanted some electrodes in the rats' brains. Each time a rat pulled a lever, the scientists stimulated the part of the rats' brains that released dopamine. They soon found out that the rats were craving dopamine so badly that they kept pulling the lever over and over for prolonged periods of time. The rats didn't care to sleep or eat any longer. They would just pull the lever until they reached exhaustion.

Next, the researchers blocked the release of dopamine in the rats' brains, which resulted in the rats becoming so lethargic that they wouldn't want to eat or drink. However, if the food was being placed in their mouths, they would eat it; only the motivation to get it themselves disappeared.

Therefore, it's not just the sensation of hunger or thirst that motivates the fulfillment of these needs, but dopamine has a key role within the process.

The experiment on rats might have been taken to an extreme, but dopamine has similar effects in our lives. Your brain will do anything to find dopamine. It will prioritize the things that will give you the highest amount of this feel-good neurotransmitter to make you feel the best. From your brain's perspective, the better you feel, the more efficient you can be for survival.

Let's take, for example, drug addicts — they are aware that drugs aren't good for them, but all they are looking for is to get more. Cocaine and heroin release exceptionally high amounts of dopamine, which eventually makes the consumers constantly crave them.

The truth is, pretty much everything releases more or less dopamine. Even drinking water when you are feeling thirsty does it. But the highest release of this feel-good chemical occurs when you get a reward randomly, like in the case of gambling.

These days, we are inundating our brains with tremendous amounts of dopamine regularly: from scrolling through social media to watching porn and binge-watching Netflix. Pay attention to your behavior and those around you. You will see how addicted we are to our phones, checking them every couple of minutes, anticipating a "like" on social media, a message, or notification. We are like those rats looking for a new dopamine dose, over and over.

Homeostasis and Allostasis

All living organisms, from plants to animals and humans, are biological systems that constantly adapt in order to maintain balance. It is necessary for survival. This ability to maintain internal balance is called homeostasis. When an imbalance occurs, there are processes triggered that have the role of bringing back equilibrium. For example, we will adapt to the temperature outside to maintain the right body heat. When we're facing hot weather, our blood vessels dilate so that more blood enters skin capillaries. We will sweat and open up our bodies so that heat is lost. When the outside temperature is low, our blood vessels constrict to reduce blood going to the skin and keep the core warm. We shiver so that the body produces heat. We curl up to reduce the surface of our bodies through which we lose heat.

Another example of homeostasis is when our blood sugar is high, the pancreas will release insulin, the body cells and liver will take up glucose, so in the end, the blood glucose level declines. Finally, the optimal glucose level in your body is achieved.

These are just two examples, but there are many processes happening in our bodies that have the role of maintaining the right level of water, nutrients, temperature, etc.

When you abuse a substance, you overstimulate certain parts of the brain. In the end, that will interfere with your body's ability to balance itself out, affecting the state of homeostasis. The brain will make adjustments by creating a new balanced set-point. This is called allostasis.

It's the reason why people who regularly drink alcohol develop tolerance, and they require a larger amount of alcohol to get drunk.

With dopamine, the process is no different. Your brain gets used to high amounts of this neurotransmitter, and the new levels become normal, so you need more to feel good. It's one of the reasons why drug addicts, even if they try to quit, find it difficult to adjust to a normal life. Their dopamine tolerance got so high that ordinary life isn't able to match it. Those addicted to social media, porn, TV, etc., experience some of the same symptoms as alcohol and drug addicts.

The things and tasks that don't give you much dopamine are perceived as boring, so it becomes more difficult to motivate yourself to do them. Right now, your brain wants you to eat comfort food, listen to music, watch TV, and anything else that gives you instant gratification.

So, what can you do to motivate yourself to do the boring, challenging activities?

The answer is simple, and it is staring at you: you need to do a dopamine detox.

How can you do a dopamine detox?

You will have to choose a day per week when you avoid all stimulating activities. You are going to let your brain and dopamine receptors recover. No fun allowed. You should use your phone and computer strictly for the necessary calls or work; if you could fully take a break from them, even better! No junk food, no TV, not any sort of feel-good stimulants. Remove all sources of external pleasure this one day. Few examples of the things you could still do in order to relax would be having a walk in nature, meditating, or exercising.

This "dopamine starvation" will have excellent benefits for you, for your motivation, productivity, and ability to achieve your goals. You will abstain from these pleasures so that your brain gets reaccustomed to lower dopamine levels, resulting in you finding those less satisfying activities more desirable.

There could also be another approach to this detox: identify your biggest addiction and give only that one up for one day a week. You can still do the other things you enjoy; just the behavior you pick will be off-limits.

You should push yourself to extend this detox as much as possible; if you could do it for two days a week, that would be great. If you could give up one behavior for an entire week, that would be amazing!

For me, a strong addiction was social media, specifically Instagram. I was wasting so much time of my day scrolling through my feed and watching random videos. But one day, I decided enough is enough, and if I wanted to achieve anything, I had to become more focused. So, I took the decision to delete the app from my phone. The first two weeks felt weird since my main source of dopamine was gone, but gradually, I forgot about it. In total, I took a six-month break from it, and it's one of the best things I've ever done. It gave me a new level of productivity, discipline and I became much happier with myself. During these six months, I needed a couple of times to use Instagram for work purposes, and I just used the desktop version. Now I've reinstalled it again on my phone because I need it sometimes for work, but I make sure I use it intentionally and not get carried away by all the cool fashion videos on the platform.

And finally, the last suggestion to increase your motivation through self-discipline is to use enjoyable activities as incentives to complete any boring tasks. For example, if you schedule eight hours of work within your day, at the end of it, allow yourself one or two hours to watch a movie, scroll through social media, or whatever makes you happy.

Super-duper important to keep in mind: if you have any damaging addictions like alcohol or cigarettes, you don't want to use them as incentives.

We're all addicted more or less to dopamine, and it's normal. But the essential part is to discipline ourselves to do the things that serve us in the long run. It's worth the effort, and later you will thank yourself for doing this!

"Easy choices, hard life. Hard choices, easy life."

— JERZY GREGOREK

Important: If you have any sort of strong drug/alcohol addiction, I recommend you seek professional help, as there is a physiological dependence, and you might experience extreme withdrawal symptoms when trying to quit the addictive substance.

Chapter 5: Key Takeaways

1. Self-doubt is most often at the root of our fear of failure. It is the reason why we don't dare to go for the things we want and often end up accepting less than we deserve.

2. Intelligent people are usually the most affected by self-doubt, thinking about all the potential negative outcomes. Courage and self-confidence are better indicators of success than intelligence.

3. Self-confidence is not a quality that we have or don't have, but a skill that can be improved throughout our lives.

4. Challenge yourself to face rejection as often as possible, as it's the only way to desensitize from the fear of it. Rejection should be used as fuel for you to become more determined to pursue your goals and not be seen as an obstacle. Go ahead and try the "10 rejections in 90 days" challenge.

5. Pay attention to the people that form your close circle of friends. How do they influence you? Do they inspire you to grow, or they hold you back from your goals? Make a first step towards joining a community of people that has similar objectives as you.

6. Your brain is wired in a way to protect you, meaning it will always try to make you avoid difficult, uncomfortable tasks. This is why you would rather spend time in front of the TV rather than working or studying.

7. Dopamine is a brain neurotransmitter that plays a crucial role in our level of motivation. The things and tasks that don't give us much dopamine, like work or study, are perceived as boring. It's difficult to motivate yourself to do them when your brain is used to high levels of dopamine. This is why it's useful to do a dopamine detox. When the brain gets reaccustomed to lower dopamine levels, those less satisfying activities will seem more desirable.

6

PRACTICAL WAYS TO DEAL WITH WORRY, FEAR, AND YOUR INNER CRITIC

"I am an old man and have known a great many troubles, but most of them never happened."

— MARK TWAIN

$\mathcal{W}$e spend more time being scared of imaginary scenarios than actually going through terrifying experiences. How much of your life have you spent worrying, and how much of it have you actually endured something bad?

Did you know that from all the things we worry about, 30% are things from the past that cannot be changed, 40% are bad scenarios that will never happen, 12% are related to people's opinion of us, 10% are related to health issues (which worry only makes worse), and only 8% are things that need us to take action? (Cox, 2015)

More than 90% of our time we spend worrying about things we have little or no control over! While we couldn't do anything else in these cases but try to be more accepting and mindful (which we'll cover in chapter 7), I shared a simple and practical method below for that 8% of worries we can act on.

Worry: How to deal with it

Worry keeps your mind in a state of blur, making you helpless in the face of problems.

To conquer your fears, you'll have to define them first!

So, please go ahead and grab a pen and paper, as you're going to need them for this strategy I'm going to show you next. Many people I know have been using this 5-step technique successfully, and obviously, I use it too when I'm worried or confused about a situation.

It's super simple and will help you get out of a fearful state by bringing more clarity over the situation you're dealing with.

1. The first step is **to think about an aspect of your life that is bothering or worrying you.** Go ahead and write it down. Determine an action step you can take to change that situation and think of the absolute worst outcome if you take that action step.

Write down in detail the most apocalyptic scenario that exists in your head: What are the things you fear? What might go wrong? What would be the consequences, and would they be irreversible? How likely would it be for your fears to happen?

Rate the magnitude of the consequences from 1 to 5 (5 being an absolute disaster, and 1 not so bad).

2. Once you're finished assessing the situation and all potential consequences of your actions, ask yourself: **Could I do something to attenuate the consequences or fix things later? If so, how would I do it?**

Searching for solutions will bring up new perspectives. When you're less busy worrying, you will be awed at your brain's capacity and creative powers to find answers.

3. The next question you need to ask yourself is: **How will your lack of action impact your life** (emotionally, physically, and financially)?

Most often, we think about what could happen if we take a particular action but forget to consider the negative consequences of inaction. In three months, six months, or a year, what would be the result of you not doing anything about this situation?

4. Accept the things that you cannot change. William James, the well-known American philosopher, and psychologist said: "Be willing to have it so. Acceptance of what has happened is the first step to overcoming the consequences of any misfortune." After you accept the worst, there is nothing else to lose.

5. Think about the potential positive outcome. Rate the benefits of a positive result, from 1-5, 5 being the best you hoped for.

For example:

1. Problem: I'm unhappy with my life, and I wish to move to another city.
What I fear will happen if I take action: I fear that I'll be completely alone at first, with nobody to count on, I might struggle financially, or I might not like it as much as I thought I would.
So, on a scale from 1-5, the negative outcome would be a 4.

2. Possible actions I could take to attenuate consequences: I could join groups online, join classes for activities I'm passionate about to connect with like-minded people. I could work a survival job initially to make ends meet. If I end up hating the city, I can move anytime somewhere else or even back to the town where I initially lived.

3. The negative consequences of inaction: I would be unhappy, and over the long term, I could end up feeling completely miserable and stuck. I could waste potential opportunities, and I would probably regret my entire life that I didn't make the change.

4. Accept the things that can't be changed: I accept that my life would be far from ideal initially, and I will start from zero on many aspects of my life.

5. The potential positive outcome: I will meet new people, discover a new city, enjoy new experiences, and find the happiness I was looking for. On a scale from 1 to 5, the positive outcome could be a 5.

Thinking about problems like this, one will realize that their fears are often not that strong, and most bad consequences could be reversible. The potential positive outcomes compared with the negative ones might be more significant, making the action step worth taking.

Dealing with Your Inner Critic

The harshest critic we will ever have will be the one inside our head. That inner voice that keeps nagging us, always whispering about our shortcomings, acts like our biggest bully. It's awfully mean for someone who doesn't really provide us with much.

Why is it so rude to us for no reason? Well, there is a reason. That inner critic we all have is trying to protect and improve us, but it doesn't always know how to do it.

Sometimes, what we say to ourselves is real. For example, if you look in the mirror and notice you've gained some weight, it's not the end of the world to point that out. It could help you to get motivated to become healthier. But if you look in the mirror and think you're disgusting and that no one will love you, then that's a problem. The deeper, hidden truth is still there – that you might need to make some healthy choices – but it's how we say it to ourselves that counts.

How you talk to yourself has a profound emotional effect. Be wary of the tone of your inner voice. Teach the voice from your head to talk more productively. Think of that inner critic like a child: you're teaching them what is appropriate to say and what is not.

If you were to learn something new, and the person teaching you would just shout and constantly criticize you, not only would it be unhelpful, but it would make you feel bad about yourself, lose your confidence and motivation. However, if they would nicely explain what's wrong and how you could improve, then the outcome would be completely different, wouldn't it?

Detach from your inner voice

What is essential to understand is that you're not your mind, and if the inside voice refuses to be nicer, there are ways to detach from it.

You don't have to listen to it just because it lives inside your head. Next time your inner voice is rude to you, you can try this:

1. Observe your critical voice, in detail on what it says to you, and its aggressive tone.
2. Stretch your arm forward with your palm up.
3. Imagine your inner voice leaving your mind and coming down inside your palm.
4. Now that it's in your palm, you can play with it: Slow it down. Change the tone to a funny one — for example, you could make it sound like a little girl or a cartoon character.

How is it? It feels less threatening, right? It's easier to brush those comments off now. This is a way to visualize that voice, so we don't let it cause so much mental damage.

Another method to apply when you can't get a particular critical thought out of your head is to try singing it. If you tell yourself, "I'm a loser, and I'll never do anything right," sing that along with your favorite song. As you start to do this, you'll realize just how silly it really sounds to say such a mean thing to yourself.

You can also try writing down your thoughts and reading them back. When you actually put your negative thoughts on paper, it helps you see them objectively and recognize just how ridiculous they are.

Be kind to yourself

"To love oneself is the beginning of a life-long romance."

— OSCAR WILDE

It's easy to love yourself on your good days, but it's essential to learn to accept yourself on your bad ones when you only see your flaws.

The base of self-compassion is self-kindness. This concept comes from the Buddhist culture and encourages us to treat ourselves as we would treat our best friend.

Accepting our flaws comes from the deep understanding we are all imperfect beings. The only perfect people that exist are those on TV and our social media feeds. But no one is as perfect as television or Instagram makes them look!

Those who struggle to show love and appreciation to themselves end up feeling a lot of internal suffering, unhappiness that leads eventually to anxiety, depression, and isolation.

Treating yourself with more kindness has many positive consequences on your well-being, making you feel inner peace, being more satisfied with your life, feeling happier and more resilient.

So, make a habit of asking yourself thoughtful questions in difficult times, same as you'd ask a friend that would need your support: How can I care for myself today? What would I say, or what advice would I give to a friend in a similar situation like this? How would I say it, most importantly?

To care for yourself when you're having a bad day, you could engage in some of your favorite activities. It can be reading, having a spa day, exercising, meditating, or spending time with family or friends. Incorporating these activities in your life when things are difficult is an excellent way of showing yourself some compassion, which will make a massive difference for your mental well-being in the long term.

Learning to put yourself first is an excellent way of self-care, especially if you continuously give time and energy to other people, forgetting to take some time for what your soul needs. From the moment you're born until the moment you die, the only person you are 100% of the time with is yourself, so try your best to make your own company and overall life journey a pleasant one. Always remember this saying by Buddha:

"You, as much as anybody in the entire Universe, deserve your love and affection."

Chapter 6: Key Takeaways

1. More than 90% of our time we spend worrying about things we have little or no control over.

2. Worry keeps your mind in a state of blur, making you helpless in the face of problems. To conquer your fears, you'll have to define them first. Apply the 5-step technique:

- Think about an aspect of your life that is bothering or worrying you. Determine an action step you can take to change that situation and think of the absolute worst outcome if you take that action step. Rate the magnitude of the consequences from 1 to 5.
- Ask yourself: Could I do something to attenuate the consequences or fix things later? If so, how would I do it?
- How will your lack of action impact your life (emotionally, physically, and financially)?
- Accept the things that you cannot change.
- Think about the potential positive outcome. Rate the benefits of a positive result, from 1-5.

Compare the ratings of the potential positive and negative outcomes and decide on whether to go ahead with your action plan or not.

3. Each time you notice you're starting to criticize yourself harshly, ask yourself how you could change that to say it in an encouraging and constructive way. Be aware of the things you say to yourself as well as the tone of your voice. Distance yourself from the voice and make it less threatening.

We all have an inner voice that criticizes us. What's essential to understand, though, is that you're not your mind, and if the inside voice refuses to be nicer, there are ways to detach from it. You can try this:

- Observe your critical voice, in detail on what it says to you, and its aggressive tone.
- Stretch your arm forward with your palm up.
- Imagine your inner voice leaving your mind and coming down inside your palm.
- Now that it's in your palm, you can play with it: Slow it down. Change the tone to a funny one. For example, you could make it sound like a little girl or a cartoon character.

Another method to apply when you can't get a particular critical thought out of your head is to try singing it. This way, you'll realize just how silly it really sounds to say such a mean thing to yourself. You can also try writing it down and reading it back in order to recognize just how ridiculous it is.

4. It's essential for our mental well-being to learn and treat ourselves better. As Buddha said:

"You, as much as anybody in the entire Universe, deserve your love and affection."

TAKE IT EASY

"You must learn in life to take things more lightly, my dear. ..."

— ELIZABETH GILBERT

𝒥 felt that this book wouldn't have been complete without a chapter dedicated to stress management techniques.

Life is meant to be enjoyed, and this section is all about finding inner balance. There are so many incredible things around us, but they often get overlooked because we get too stuck in our heads.

Stress management techniques improve our mental wellbeing, making us feel relaxed and happy from the inside. They should be a consistent practice in our lives, just like brushing our teeth or washing our hair.

Unmanaged stress can have an immense negative impact on your health and energy levels. If you don't press the pause button once in a while, you will burn yourself out. Taking a step back and learning how to lower your stress levels will help you create a happy inner life that will reflect in your external world.

In this chapter, I've shared my top 5 favorite practices that I've been using for the past 15 years, which helped me maintain my inner balance and mental wellbeing in times of stress.

These practices are: mindfulness, daily intention, breathing exercises, spending time in nature, and gratitude practice.

1. Mindfulness

"In a world full of doing, doing, doing, it's important to take a moment to just breathe, to just be."

— UNKNOWN

Mindfulness is one of the most popular types of meditation that teaches us stillness, to enjoy the present moment. It is a mental state we achieve when we focus on being in the moment while calmly acknowledging and accepting our thoughts, feelings, and bodily sensations.

When practicing mindfulness, you allow your emotions and feelings to come up without placing any judgement on them. Just like a focus object, mindfulness pulls you from your deepest inner thoughts and places you right in the present. When you're trapped in the cells of your mental prison, it may seem like there is no way out. Mindfulness releases all the negative thoughts you have, so you become able to enjoy what's in front of you. It teaches you to just be.

Simple activities like walking through the woods, gardening, washing the dishes, or playing an instrument can be acts of mindfulness. As you are doing these activities, your mind should be focused on completing them, leaving no more room for worries.

Below I've shared three simple exercises you can use to practice mindfulness:

The focus exercise. Start by choosing an object that you have handy. It can be a piece of clothing you wear, something you are eating, or anything else from your room. You will need to place your entire focus on that object and observe it: How does it look like? How does its texture feel like? How does it smell? Examine it with your entire being and allow yourself to be absorbed by every little detail. By doing so, your mind won't be able to drift off any longer.

The five senses. This mindfulness activity helps you to travel through each of your senses. Start first by identifying five things you can see. You don't have to do anything with these objects. You don't have to pick them up, touch them, or walk to them. Simply pick them out with your vision. After that, pick four things that you can touch. Again, you don't have to actually stand up and touch these things. You don't have to hold them. Just envision them and what they might feel like. Think about a soft couch across the room. Think about a cat. Think about the sink in the kitchen and how it feels to wash your hands. Pick out these four objects and fully let your mind envision what it is like to touch them.

Third, pick out three things that you hear. It might be somebody chatting in the other room. It could be as simple as the air conditioner running. Next, pick out two things that you can smell. Again, you don't need to be able to smell them right now. You can just picture what they smell like. For example, think about the tree outside your window and how it smells. Think about the food you have in the fridge and what that smells like. Finally, pick one thing you can taste. Think about what it feels like to eat it and how you might consume it. By traveling through these five senses, you're reconnecting to your body. This technique will help reduce your stress and alleviate built-up tension.

You can incorporate the five-sense activity in your daily life. For instance, cooking is a wonderful activity for mindfulness. First, you touch everything that you will be cooking with. You have to figure out what pots, pans, mixing bowls, and utensils are required to complete the meal. Next, you start chopping and cooking, meaning you will be able to smell the food. You have to engage your hearing as well — listen to the sizzling sound, for example. The whole time your mind is focused on the food you're cooking, and when it's all done, you get to taste it!

Not every activity will be as sensory as cooking, but other practices that help focus your mind this way are great for alleviating anxiety. When you're painting, you look at the canvas, touch the brushes, and smell the paint. When gardening, you're touching the dirt, smelling the flowers, and hearing the buzz of animals and bugs outside. The point is to keep you mentally absorbed to prevent your mind from traveling into deep, dark places.

Body Scan. A body scan is a wonderful mindfulness activity that involves paying attention to different parts of your body, in a gradual sequence, from head to toes. To make the most out of this exercise, find a place that you can lay down and begin to relax. Stretch your body out, and don't bend it or strain any muscles. Find a place that is quiet as well, so you don't have any noise disturbing you. Breathe in through your nose and out through your mouth. During the body scan, travel down each part of your body. Focus on your head, your ears, your eyes, your nose, your lips, your tongue, and your throat. With every breath that you take in and out, you focus on a different part of your body. Travel down to your shoulders and your chest, your back, your arms, your elbows, your fingers, and your wrists. Focus on your stomach, your lungs, your heart, and everything else in your torso. Finally, travel through your legs and your toes.

Whenever you're feeling anxious, you can focus on going through each of these areas of your anatomy. It helps to pull you back into the moment while also staying connected to your body.

2. Your daily intention

Practicing daily intention is very powerful. Every day you wake up, take few minutes to set one intention for that day and write it down. Keep in mind that a daily intention is different than setting a daily goal. A daily intention is something you live by throughout your day, rather than something you're looking to achieve and cross off your checklist. It should be more like guidance. Few examples of daily intentions are: to maintain a serene attitude no matter what happens, to act with courage, to be productive, to go out from your comfort zone on as many occasions as possible, to focus on healthy eating, to connect more with those around you, to spread positive energy, to be mindful the entire day, etc. The choice is all yours. You can't go wrong with this, as long as whatever intention you choose puts you in a positive headspace. Always keep it in the back of your mind. It might help if you would write it on a post-it note and place it on your desk. You are going to act with that in mind, creating the day you intended for yourself, no matter the circumstances. Having this daily intention will help keep you focused on who you want to be and what you want to achieve long term.

3. Breathing Exercises

Breath has a powerful effect on our physical and emotional state. Have you noticed how you breathe when you are feeling calm? How about when you are stressed and tense? If you haven't, make sure you pay attention in the future and notice how different the body feels — for example, in the morning when you just wake up, take the time to observe how relaxed your breathing is, how there's no tension in your body.

Our physiology has a very strong influence on our inner state. When we change our posture, the way we breathe, our facial expression, we will influence how we feel inside, which will ultimately impact our behavior.

If you don't believe me, try this right now: take a few deep, relaxing breaths and put a large smile on your face. Keep smiling for 15 seconds. Your inner state just changed for the better, right?

The common belief is that what happens in the outside world affects our behavior, but the inside has a stronger impact. The truth is, in the short period between the moment when something happens externally and our reaction, our physiology changes. Ultimately it has the biggest influence on how we feel and act.

Now, back to breathing. The way we breathe affects our entire body, so breathing exercises will help remove any tension you might be feeling. They are easy to practice and don't require any sort of equipment. I've included in this section three breathing exercises: belly breathing, 3-6-9 breathing, and color breathing.

Belly breathing: is one of the easiest and best breathing exercises to start with as a beginner.

- Pick a place where you can sit or lie down comfortably. Place one hand on your belly and the other one on your chest.
- Take a deep breath through the nose. While doing that, your belly should push your hand out, while the chest will stay unmoved.
- Keep the air in for few seconds.
- Breathe out slowly through your mouth and feel the hand on the belly going down; use it to push the air out gently.
- Repeat for few times until you feel calm, and all tension is removed from the body.

The second breathing exercise is a bit more advanced and is called the **3-6-9 breathing**.

- Pick a place where you can sit or lie down comfortably. Place one hand on your belly and the other one on your chest.
- Take a deep breath through the nose. While doing that, your belly should push your hand out, while the chest will stay unmoved. Placing your hand on your stomach helps to ground you and reconnect you with your body.
- Breath in for 3 seconds.
- Hold your breath for 6 seconds.
- Breath out through your mouth for 9 seconds, releasing all the anxiety that built up inside you.
- Repeat for few times until you feel calm.

And the last exercise is **color breathing**.

- Choose a place where you can sit or lie down comfortably.
- Breath in and out while visualizing a color of your choice and let it wash over you.
- Picture it traveling through your bloodstream and coming out through the air that you breathe. Fill yourself with this color. If you're choosing a relaxing color like blue or purple, it can help you calm down. If you want to get energized, you might want to choose a color like orange or yellow.

It's easy to get lost in our minds. Therefore, the physical vessels we have on this Earth are so important to stay connected to. Our lungs are capable of controlling our entire body when we practice breathing. The more you utilize this ability, the more control you have over your relaxation. Remember to also not force breathing too fast. If you're doing it too hard, straining yourself, you might end up feeling lightheaded or even more anxious afterwards.

4. Go out in nature

This stress management practice has such an energizing power and is the simplest thing one can do: go out and spend some time in nature. Nature can instantly take you to the present moment. Its beauty makes you pay full attention to it. Notice the sounds of the animals, the birds that chirp, the sound of the wind. Grab a leaf from the ground and feel its texture. Breath in the fresh air. Look up to the sky and enjoy the rays of sun falling on your face or have fun looking at the odd shapes of the clouds.

5. Gratitude practice

The practice of gratitude has become very popular only in the last few years, even though the principles on which it is based go hundreds of years back. Most religions and spiritual practices encourage people to practice gratitude in one way or another. It's a principle so simple but with such a powerful effect. Those who regularly practice it experience a better quality of life, having better energy, feeling more compassionate, and excited about life.

Some people think that gratitude should be expressed when something amazing happens in their lives. While that is wonderful, gratitude is not only about that. It is about looking for reasons to be grateful even in the ordinary or awful days.

I started practicing gratitude a few years back, and the truth is, there are still weeks when I struggle to feel grateful. But, even if it takes me a bit, I always find something. It's easy to forget about the great things we have when we get trapped in the whirlwind of life.

Following his research, psychologist Robert Emmons and author of "Thanks!: How the new science of gratitude can make you happier", concluded that keeping a gratitude journal about the things we appreciate improves our life satisfaction drastically.

Too often, we get focused on what we don't have, as well as the things we are hoping to gain. For example, even if you have a great partner, you get unhappy that you don't have your own house; If you have a great home and a great partner, you're not fully satisfied because you want a work promotion. And so on. When you look for a reason to be dissatisfied – guess what – you'll always find one. But the point is to look for the positive things that already exist in your life. You will always want to get more. It's human nature to want to grow and develop, but you shouldn't allow this desire to make you feel unhappy.

Start practicing gratitude every day. You can do it in the morning or at night if you prefer. I do it before I go to bed. I try to think about three good things from that day: maybe I had a nice cup of coffee, perhaps I took some time to chat with a good friend, or I've spent time with family. It can be anything. We have so many things to be grateful for.

We shouldn't appreciate only the positive aspects of our lives, but the negative experiences too, that most probably have taught us some valuable lessons. It's not like we enjoy these poor experiences or that we would actively choose to live through them again, but they hold great value. We have to live through those dark moments to fully appreciate the light of the good ones. Accepting life's negative parts is the kind of attitude that will create more internal peace and adaptability, so when a big wave of discomfort comes, we will have the skills to ride it out.

Since the benefits of gratitude practice are so great, you would think it's enough reason for us to make it a habit. But in reality, the majority of people that start practicing it stop only a few days later. After the initial excitement is gone, people lose motivation and see it more as a chore. So, a few helpful tactics you can apply to keep things exciting and turn this into a long-term practice are:

- Be specific with your thanks. Even though "I'm grateful for the city I live in" might make you feel good for a day or two, you'll realize its effects will start to fade away. So, be specific exactly what you are grateful for regarding your city, for example, "I'm grateful for the park next to my house, as it makes me feel re-energized and happy". Also, adding some variety to your journal will help keep it interesting and freshen up those feelings of gratitude. Try each day to find three new reasons to be grateful for. Make it a fun game by noticing new awesome things.

- Usually, people pick either the morning or the night to do their gratitude practice. If you chose to do this in the morning but then realize you'd rather sleep in for ten more minutes, you should better choose another time of the day. Gratitude journaling shouldn't be a chore. It should be enjoyable and make you feel good. I sometimes do it when I commute; sometimes, I take time during my lunch break. These variations help me not get bored of it.

- The gratitude journal shouldn't necessarily be as boring as filing in a notebook. A more exciting, fun way to do it is to create a gratitude jar: when feeling grateful about a particular thing, write it down on a little piece of paper and put it in a jar. At the end of the year, you can empty it and review the things you wrote. Also, you could send a gratitude note to someone you feel grateful for. Keeping it fun is essential in making this a long-lasting habit. One of the things that influence most our motivation is autonomy or the ability to do the things we want, so keep it interesting!

Don't take for granted the amazing things and people that exist in your life. Pay attention and express your gratitude for the smallest, simple things. Thank the Universe /God or any other spiritual force you believe in, for everything: for your body because it is doing so many amazing things for you, for your family, your friends, your mind, your hands which hold the ones you love, your feet because they carry you to so many beautiful places on this Earth, for sunrise and moon and stars, for happiness, for pain because it makes you stronger, and don't forget to be thankful for your fears too, because you get to know so many growth opportunities.

Chapter 7: Key Takeaways

1. Considering the levels of stress we face these days, stress management techniques are essential for our mental wellbeing. They should be a consistent practice in our lives, just like brushing our teeth or washing our hair.

2. The top 5 recommended stress management practices are: mindfulness, daily intention, breathing exercises, time in nature, and gratitude practice.

3. Mindfulness teaches us stillness and to enjoy the present. We focus on being in the moment while calmly acknowledging our feelings, thoughts, and bodily sensations.The focus exercise, the five senses, and the body scan are three great mindfulness exercises.

4. Setting a daily intention each morning will keep you committed to your goals and put you in a positive headspace.

5. Our physiology is very powerful. The body posture, breathing, or facial expressions will influence how we feel inside, which eventually will alter our behavior. In the brief period, from the moment when something happens in the outside world to when we react, our physiology changes. Ultimately it has the biggest impact on how we feel and act.

6. Breathing exercises are a powerful method to release tension from your body. Try belly breathing, 3-6-9 breathing, and color breathing.

7. Nature has a great energizing power. Its beauty helps us to stay present. Whenever we feel the need to recharge, some time in nature is always a good idea.

8. The practice of gratitude can improve your life satisfaction drastically. You should make it a daily habit by taking few minutes each day to count your blessings. Keep it fun by adding variations to it, so it doesn't start feeling like a chore.

LEAVE A 1-CLICK REVIEW!

Hey, you almost finished this read. Amazing job! Most people start a book but never finish it, so give yourself a pat on the back.

Before wrapping up, I just wanted to say that I would really appreciate if you could take few short seconds to **leave an honest review on Amazon.** As a self-publisher, I rely on the feedback and support of my readers.

To make things fast and easy, simply scan the QR code below, which will take you straight to the review link:

CONCLUSION

Our time here on this planet is short. There is no time to waste it by living in fear. You have a unique potential that is all going to waste when you doubt yourself and don't dare to go for your goals. This is not to say you shouldn't feel fear. Fear is what makes us humans. As Nelson Mandela said:

"I learned that courage was not the absence of fear, but the triumph over it."

My fears crippled me for most of my life. I've spent so much time in soul-crushing jobs because I was scared to make a change and doubted my capabilities. I used to hate the life I was having, and eventually, I got depressed. I remember saying to myself many times that I didn't want to live any longer if that's how life was supposed to be – a constant struggle to make ends meet, feeling no fulfillment and no joy. I didn't see any light at the end of the tunnel. It took me a while until I found my way out, but it was worth it. I tried and failed and then failed some more. There have been many times when I wanted to give up, but I'm glad I haven't. Even if I didn't realize it at the time, I was very lucky that my circumstances forced me to go all-in in my search for purpose and fulfillment. When you have nothing more to lose, you have everything to gain. I didn't have the luxury to accept a defeat. It was a go-hard or go-home situation.

It breaks my heart now to see people that choose comfort and unhappiness over uncertainty. And that's why I decided to create this book and send my message to as many people as possible. There's so much life has to offer, but all of it has got a price, and you need to honestly ask yourself if you're willing to pay it through hard work, consistency, and dedication. "Success is going from disappointment to disappointment without losing enthusiasm", as Winston Churchill said.

We need to learn the difference between the moments when fear protects us and when fear holds us down. Stop telling yourself why you can't do something and start asking yourself how you can do it. Ask yourself if you're making a decision because you really think it is the best one or you're taking it out of fear because you avoid something? Life is made up of choices.

Each decision, big or small, contributes to the shape of your future.

Steve Jobs said:

"Your time is limited, so don't waste it living someone else's life. Don't be trapped by dogma, which is living with the results of other people's thinking. Don't let the noise of others' opinions drown out your inner voice. And most important, have the courage to follow your heart and intuition."

Go out and try. Make mistakes, fail, accept you are terrible in the beginning. And be stubborn. Stubborn enough to never quit trying, refuse to listen to anyone saying you can't do it.

Each day is a perfect day to start again, to reinvent yourself. To fall and get back up. Don't misjudge difficulties with being bad at something, as this framing will affect your sense of self-worth. You need adversity to find out what you're capable of. Your difficulties are an opportunity to grow and not a sign for you to stop. Change your perspective on what it means to fail. Look up your heroes and remind yourself that even the most successful people on the planet had moments in their past when they failed. Their failures led them further to success.

It's enough to do something better than you did yesterday. Progress doesn't have to be spectacular. But you need to commit to trusting and loving yourself no matter what.

Start by diving deep into your mind. There's a reason we try to avoid failure as much as possible. When we prevent ourselves from making mistakes, it gives us the chance to sustain our ego. Potential judgement from others can be scary, so we want to protect our image by avoiding mistakes in the first place. Our core fears reveal deeper reasons for wanting to procrastinate.

Getting stuck in your head can be the quickest road to failure. Free yourself from the restraints of your mind. Overthinking can be paralyzing. Making the right decision will always present a certain difficulty, but for the most part, we have to just bite the bullet and decide.

Challenge your thoughts and figure out where they came from. Finding out their source will give you a different perspective, helping you see things as they are and not having to project your fears or past experiences.

Let go of perfectionism. Striving to be the best you can is important and will lead you to great achievements. But fixating on small details and putting all your attention in the wrong places will leave you chasing fantasies. Confront the pains that make you want to procrastinate head-on. At least follow through with the bare minimum. When everything feels like it's piling on, it's better to do a small thing rather than nothing at all.

Drop your ego and accept there is so much to learn still. Everybody has big dreams of doing something great in life, but not all people are willing to take criticism and look at what they are doing wrong. This type of mentality will hinder any chance at success.

One of the most popular myths in this world says that talent has a decisive saying on the level of achievement one obtains. I don't contest the fact that each person has a predisposition to be good at one thing more than another. That is very true. But talent holds at most 1% of the weight, while the rest of 99% is consistency and dedication.

Most people prefer to believe that God-given talent has the final say in achieving something extraordinary because, this way, they have an excuse to not work hard enough.

Regardless of their talent, all the greats of this world overcame incredible amounts of adversity and put in thousands of hours of work and dedication. Your willingness to put in the required effort is going to separate you from the mediocre crowd. It is not easy to achieve greatness, and it doesn't happen overnight, but you can make it happen. It is all in your hands. You are capable of becoming anything that you want to become. The only question is: Are you willing to pay the price to get there?

Will you allow fear to define you, or will you choose to push through until you succeed?

No matter how talented you are, if you let others outwork you and be more perseverant than you, they are going to outperform you in the long run.

The mindset you have is the number one factor that will decide whether you achieve your goals. Watch your daily thoughts. As the great philosopher Marcus Aurelius said: "Our lives are what our thoughts make it". If we think fearful thoughts, we will be fearful. If we think about failure, we will bring it into existence. We are shaped by what we hold in our minds. Decide on who you want to become, and no matter how difficult, uncomfortable that feels at first, go through the process of repetition and shaping yourself the way that a sculptor creates his final work of art, little by little and day after day.

The English poet John Milton used to say:

"The mind is its own place, and in itself can make a heaven of hell, a hell of heaven."

We are not hurt that much by external events as we are by our thoughts and opinions over what happened. Our reaction is in our powers. Growing your mindset allows you to see things in a new light.

Evaluating the people you surround yourself with is important to determine how you might be influenced. If you don't believe in yourself, how can you expect anyone else to?

Take the time to get to know yourself, your passions, abilities, strengths, and shortcomings. Take the decision to live your life and learn to stop comparing yourself to others. You were not born to live their life, so there's no point in wasting time being jealous of their journey and what they have.

Don't let the negative experiences from your past determine your future life. Don't stay stuck in the same pattern of living that you've been in for years. Start again as many times as you need.

In his well-known book "How to Stop worrying and start living, " Dale Carnegie told the story of a teacher named Paul Brandwine. One day, in one of his classes, Brandwine made a demonstration to his students, which taught them an important life lesson — one they were never going to forget. He grabbed a bottle of milk and knocked it over, so all of it spilled down the drain. He asked his students to come closer and look at the spilt milk and told them: "I want you to remember this lesson for the rest of your lives. That milk is gone. You can see it down the drain; all the fussing and hair-pulling in the world won't bring back a drop of it. With a little thought and prevention, that milk might have been saved. But it's too late now. All we can do is write it off, forget it and go on to the next thing."

We, as humans, deal too often with the "I should have" and "I shouldn't have" kinds of thoughts. Even if it happened a second ago, what's done is done, and we shouldn't waste any other second regretting it. We all make mistakes. We make decisions we regret, and we say things that we shouldn't have said. There is no way you could predict all the possible outcomes. Life has no "undo" button, so there's no time for regret. Stop dwelling on your past mistakes. Come to terms with your past actions and focus on the present so you can improve the future. Instead of wishing things to be different, concentrate on finding a way to make them different.

You can't find out what you're truly made of if you keep looking at your past. As Steve Maraboli said:

"We all make mistakes, have struggles, and even regret things in our past. But you are not your mistakes, you are not your struggles, and you are here, now with the power to shape your day and your future."

Be proud of yourself for being willing to take risks. Most people fail because they're not willing to put themselves out there, to try, to be embarrassed, to be bad. They avoid failure, and this is why they fail. Stop trying to avoid pain. If you're committed to doing something great, you need to know pain comes in the same package that achievement does. You have to educate yourself to seek discomfort and challenges because pain is the best motivating factor that will push you to take action.

Regardless of your circumstances, all that matters is how much you're willing to learn and how much you are willing to fall and get back up.

Finally, remember to take it easy. Life is short. It will zoom by you before you know it, so you'd better have some fun and not take it that seriously. Within your journey of trying to achieve your goals, don't forget you're doing it to create a better life. So, have fun once in a while. And stay grateful. It's easy to lose appreciation for the good things around you when you take them for granted, therefore make a habit of counting your blessings.

Lastly, if you were to forget everything you read in this book, at least remember these three things:

1. If you don't go after what you want, you will never have it.
2. If you don't ask, the answer is always no.
3. If you don't step forward, you'll always be in the same place. (Roberts, n.d)

These rules have really helped me stay focused on the right direction, so I always have them in the back of my mind and live life by them as much as possible.

And before we wrap up, I have a confession to make. This book is the first one that I ever wrote. It might be good, it might be bad (I can't judge my own work objectively, so I'll let you, my reader, give me feedback), but I am willing to put it out there and see it as a starting point from which I can grow. I know that I've done the best of my abilities to do a decent job with it, so it can be helpful, motivating, inspirational and relatable to all my readers. And most importantly, I've written it from the heart!

I trust that you will use the information from this book with success, push the boundaries of fear on each occasion and try to make the best out of your time here, on planet Earth.

XX
Wilda

Just for you!
A FREE GIFT

As a way to thank you for your purchase, you will be getting the "12 tips & tricks to help you become a better and faster decision maker" eBook for free :) Click <u>HERE</u> to access your gift or go to www.wildahale.com

REFERENCES

Adams, R. L. (2016). *21 Famous Failures Who Refused to Give Up*. Huff Post. https://www.huffpost.com/entry/21-famous-failures-who-refused-to-give-up

Aiken, C. (2017). *Overthinking - A habit that fuels depression*. Mood Treatment Center. https://www.moodtreatmentcenter.com/rumination.pdf

Albrecht, K. (2012, March 22). *The (Only) 5 Fears We All Share*. Psychology Today. https://www.psychologytoday.com/us/blog/brainsnacks/201203/the-only-5-fears-we-all-share

Allerhand, R. (2019). *How to overcome fear of failure*. Net Doctor. https://www.netdoctor.co.uk/healthy-living/mental-health/a26821636/fear-of-failure/#:~:text=Also%20-known%20as%20atychiphobia%2C%20fear,of%20failing%20can%20be%20paralysing

Atychiphobia – definition, pronunciation, causes, sign, symptoms, test, treatments. (n.d.). Drugs Details. https://drugsdetails.com/atychiphobia-definition-pronunciation-causes-sign-symptoms-test-treatments/

B, A. (2017, June 22). *THE GROWTH MINDSET – THE POWER OF YET.* Nobel Coaching. https://nobelcoaching.com/growth-mindset-power-yet/

Bergland, C. (2017). *Can't Do It Perfectly? Just Do It, Badly!* Psychology Today. https://www.psychologytoday.com/intl/blog/the-athletes-way/201709/cant-do-it-perfectly-just-do-it-badly

Bergland, C. (2018a). *Is the Perfectionism Plague Taking a Psychological Toll?* Psychology Today. https://www.psychologytoday.com/intl/blog/the-athletes-way/201801/is-the-perfectionism-plague-taking-psychological-toll

Bergland, C. (2018b). *Self-Compassion Counterbalances Maladaptive Perfectionism.* Psychology Today. https://www.psychologytoday.com/intl/blog/the-athletes-way/201802/self-compassion-counterbalances-maladaptive-perfectionism

Bergland, C. (2018c, January 5). *Five Ways to Overcome Fear of Failure and Perfectionism.* Psychology Today. https://www.psychologytoday.com/intl/blog/the-athletes-way/201801/five-ways-overcome-fear-failure-and-perfectionism

Bernhard, T. (2018). *How to Overcome Your Perfectionist Tendencies*. Psychology Today. https://www.psychologytoday.com/us/blog/turning-straw-gold/201806/how-overcome-your-perfectionist-tendencies

Bokhari, D. (n.d.). *Action leads to motivation*. Dean Bokhari. https://www.deanbokhari.com/acton-leads-motivation/

British Psychological Society. (2014, September 21). *Fear of failure from a young age affects attitude to learning*. Science Daily. https://www.sciencedaily.com/releases/2014/09/140921223559.htm

Burkus, D. (2018, May 23). *You're NOT The Average Of The Five People You Surround Yourself With*. Medium. https://medium.com/the-mission/youre-not-the-average-of-the-five-people-you-surround-yourself-with-f21b817f6e69

Campbell, S. (2017, November 30). *6 Ways to Develop a Growth Mindset*. Entrepreneur. https://www.entrepreneur.com/article/305335

Carpenter, D. (n.d.). *The Science Behind Gratitude (and How It Can Change Your Life)*. Happify. https://www.happify.com/hd/the-science-behind-gratitude/#:~:text=People%20who%20regularly%20prac-tice%20gratitude,even%20have%20stronger%20immune%20systems

Choua, C. (n.d.). *60 Things to Be Grateful For In Life*. Tiny Buddha. https://tinybuddha.com/blog/60-things-to-be-grateful-for-in-life/

Clifford, C. (2020, May 22). *Jeff Bezos to exec after product totally flopped: 'You can't, for one minute, feel bad.'* CNBC. https://www.cnbc.com/2020/05/22/jeff-bezos-why-you-cant-feel-bad-about-failure.html

Coggshall, V. (n.d.). *Scared to Try: Moving Beyond the Paralysis of Perfectionism*. Tiny Buddha. Retrieved July 29, 2020, from https://tinybuddha.com/blog/scared-to-try-moving-beyond-the-paralysis-of-perfectionism/

Cox, M. (2015). *Stress, worry and faith* [Slides]. Slideshare. https://www.slideshare.net/mccx/stress-worry-and-faith

Dopamine. (n.d.). Psychology Today. https://www.psychologytoday.com/us/basics/dopamine

Falconer, J. (2020). *How to Use Parkinson's Law to Get More Done in Less Time*. Life Hack. https://www.lifehack.org/articles/featured/how-to-use-parkinsons-law-to-your-advantage.html

Fearless Motivation. (2017). *Surround Yourself With People Who Will Lift You Higher*. https://www.fearlessmotivation.com/2017/07/25/surround-yourself-with-people-who-will-lift-you-higher/

Ferguson, C. (n.d.). *How Your Mind Works and Why It's Important To Know.* Caroline Ferguson. https://carolineferguson.com/how-your-mind-works/

Ferrari, M., Yap, K., Scott, N., Einstein, D. A., & Ciarrochi, J. (2018). *Self-compassion moderates the perfectionism and depression link in both adolescence and adulthood.* NCBI. https://www.ncbi.nlm.nih.gov/pmc/articles/PMC5821438/

Ferris, T. (2017). *Fear-Setting: The Most Valuable Exercise I Do Every Month.* Tim Blog. https://tim.blog/2017/05/15/fear-setting/

Fishel, B. (2017). *How to stop rumination.* Project Monkey Mind. http://www.projectmonkeymind.com/2017/09/how-to-stop-ruminating/

Flam, F. (2016). *If You're So Smart, Why Aren't You Rich?* Bloomberg. https://www.bloomberg.com/opinion/articles/2016-12-22/if-you-re-so-smart-why-aren-t-you-rich

Focus Booster. (n.d.). *The pomodoro technique.* Focus Booster App. Retrieved August 1, 2020, from https://www.focusboosterapp.com/the-pomodoro-technique

Fritscher, L. (2020). *What is fear?* Very Well Mind. https://www.verywellmind.com/the-psychology-of-fear-2671696

Good Reads. (n.d.). *Les Brown Quotes.* https://www.goodreads.com/quotes/884712-the-graveyard-is-the-richest-place-on-earth-because-it

Goodyear, M. (n.d.). *Why I Won't Let the Fear of Failure Hold Me Back*. Tiny Buddha. Retrieved August 1, 2020, from https://tinybuddha.com/blog/why-i-wont-let-the-fear-of-failure-hold-me-back/

Green, A. (2017). *Don't Cry Over Spilt Milk*. Medium. https://medium.com/@adamgreen_64016/dont-cry-over-spilt-milk-6f2bf678ff22

Gura, L. (2014, January 24). *Fear Of Failure*. Actualized. https://www.actualized.org/articles/fear-of-failure

Hadden, J. (2020). *Why Aren't More Highly Intelligent People Rich? A Nobel Prize-Winning Economist Says Another Factor Matters a Lot More*. INC. https://www.inc.com/jeff-haden/why-arent-more-highly-intelligent-people-rich-a-novel-prize-winning-economist-says-another-factor-matters-a-lot-more.html

Hartney, E. (2020). *How Does Addiction Change Homeostasis?* Very Well Mind. https://www.verywellmind.com/definition-of-homeostasis-22207

Healthline Editorial Team. (2017). *5 Steps for Overcoming Indecision*. Healthline. https://www.healthline.com/health/5-steps-overcoming-indecision#why-is-it-hard

Healthwise Staff. (2019). *Stress Management: Breathing Exercises for Relaxation*. UOFM Health. https://www.uofmhealth.org/health-library/uz2255#:~:text=Breath-

ing%20exercises%20can%20help%20you,to%20-
calm%20down%20and%20relax

Hill, A. P., & Curran, T. (2017). *Perfectionism is increasing over time: A meta-analysis of birth cohort differences from 1989 to 2016.* American Psychological Association. https://psycnet.apa.org/doiLanding?doi=10.1037%2Fbul0000138

Hoomans, J. (2015, March 20). *35,000 Decisions: The Great Choices of Strategic Leaders.* Go Roberts. https://go.roberts.edu/leadingedge/the-great-choices-of-strategic-leaders#:~:text=Various%20internet%20sources%20estimate%20that,%26%20Labuzetta%2C%202013)

Horvath, T., Misra, K., Epner, A. K., & Cooper, G. M. (n.d.). *How Does Addiction Affect the Brain?* Center Site. https://www.centersite.net/poc/view_doc.php?type=doc&id=48370&cn=1408

How to Be. (2020, June 9). *How I Tricked My Brain To Like Doing Hard Things (dopamine detox)* [Video]. YouTube. https://www.youtube.com/watch?v=ll0OIOJz8es

Investopedia. (2020). *Pareto Principle.* https://www.investopedia.com/terms/p/paretoprinciple.asp

Japanahome. (2020). *Wabi-Sabi: How To Embrace This Ancient Japanese Philosophy At Home And Life?* https://japanahome.com/journal/wabi-sabi-how-to-embrace-this-ancient-japanese-philosophy-at-home-and-life/

John Spencer. (2017, March 27). *Growth Mindset vs. Fixed Mindset* [Video]. YouTube. https://www.youtube.com/watch?v=M1CHPnZfFmU

Kane, B. (n.d.). *The Science of Analysis Paralysis.* Doist. Retrieved July 16, 2020, from https://blog.doist.com/analysis-paralysis-productivity/

Kaufman, J. (n.d.). *What Is 'Parkinson's Law'?* Personal MBA. https://personalmba.com/parkinsons-law/

Levin, M. (n.d.). *5 Lessons Learned From 100 Days of Rejection.* INC. https://www.inc.com/marissa-levin/5-lessons-learned-from-100-days-of-rejection.html

Maclin, A. (2011). *6 Steps to Stop Overthinking Your Life.* Real Simple. https://www.realsimple.com/work-life/life-strategies/get-over-overthinking

McIntyre, G. (2020, November 20). *What Is the Small Business Failure Rate?* Fundera. https://www.fundera.com/blog/what-percentage-of-small-businesses-fail#:~:text=What%20Is%20the%20Small%20Business,their%2010th%20year%20in%20business.

McKenna, P. (2004). *Change your life in 7 days.* Litera.

Mindfulness. (n.d.). Lexico. https://www.lexico.com/definition/mindfulness

Moline, P. (2015, October 31). *We're far more afraid of failure than ghosts: Here's how to stare it down.* LA Times. https://www.latimes.com/health/la-he-scared-20151031-story.html#:~:text=Fear%20and%20exhilaration%20do%20go,even%20the%20paranormal%20(15%25).

Morin, A. (2017, April 24). *6 Ways to Stop Overthinking Everything.* Inc. https://www.inc.com/amy-morin/6-ways-to-stop-overthinking-everything.html?cid=search

Morin, A. (2018). *The Simple but Effective Way to Stop Worrying So Much.* INC. https://www.inc.com/amy-morin/the-simple-but-effective-way-to-stop-worrying-so-much-it-sounds-ridiculous-but-it-actually-works.html?cid=search

Morin, A. (2019). *10 Signs You're an Overthinker.* INC. https://www.inc.com/amy-morin/10-signs-you-think-too-much-and-what-you-can-do-about-it.html

Newman, L. (n.d.). *10 Ways Creativity Can Completely Change Your Life.* Tiny Buddha. Retrieved August 3, 2020, from https://tinybuddha.com/blog/10-ways-creativity-can-completely-change-your-life/

Ohio University. (2018). *The Six-Hour Workday.* Online Masters Ohio. https://onlinemasters.ohio.edu/blog/benefits-of-a-shorter-work-week/

Oppong, T. (2016, September 25). *Stop Waiting for The Perfect Time. There isn't One!* Medium. https://medium.com/

the-mission/stop-waiting-for-the-perfect-time-there-isnt-one-249e2f9e34fb

Oppong, T. (2018). *Wabi-Sabi: The Japanese Philosophy For a Perfectly Imperfect Life*. Medium. https://medium.com/personal-growth/wabi-sabi-the-japanese-philosophy-for-a-perfectly-imperfect-life-11563e833dc0

Perell, D. (2018, February 7). *Social media gives us a false impression of the success of others* [Tweet]. Twitter. https://twitter.com/david_perell/status/961322027817762816?s=21

Perfectionism. (n.d.). Psychology Today. https://www.psychologytoday.com/intl/basics/perfectionism

Pham, T. (2016). *The story of how Jia Jiang conquered his fear of rejection and the lessons he learned along the way.* The Hustle. https://thehustle.co/100-days-of-rejection-therapy-can-make-you-fearless

Pogosyan, M. (2018, February 2). *Be Kind to Yourself.* Psychology Today. https://www.psychologytoday.com/us/blog/between-cultures/201802/be-kind-yourself

Polivy, J., Herman, C. P., & Deo, R. (n.d.). *Getting a bigger slice of the pie. Effects on eating and emotion in restrained and unrestrained eaters.* Science Direct. Retrieved July 29, 2020, from https://www.sciencedirect.com/science/article/abs/pii/S0195666310004630

Quote Investigator. (n.d.). *Success Is Never Final and Failure Never Fatal. It's Courage That Counts.* Retrieved August 5, 2020, from https://quoteinvestigator.com/2013/09/03/success-final/#note-7156-6

Racine, N. (2019, April 1). *From Playgrounds to College: Failure Helps Build Kids' Resilience.* The Epoch Times. https://www.theepochtimes.com/from-playgrounds-to-college-failure-helps-build-kids-resilience_2850751.html

Raff, J., & Khazan, O. (2016). *How to Turn Anxiety Into Excitement.* The Atlantic. https://www.theatlantic.com/video/index/485297/turn-anxiety-into-excitement/

Raypole, C. (2020). *How to Beat 'Analysis Paralysis' and Make All the Decisions.* Healthline. https://www.healthline.com/health/mental-health/analysis-paralysis#self-confidence

Reber, P. (2010, May 1). *What Is the Memory Capacity of the Human Brain?* Scientific American. https://www.scientificamerican.com/article/what-is-the-memory-capacity/#:~:text=You%20might%20have%20only%20a, (or%20a%20million%20gigabytes).

Renee Amberg. (2018, September 26). *10 MINDFUL EXERCISES | How To Be Present | RENEE AMBERG* [Video]. YouTube. https://www.youtube.com/watch?v=SuSLOdgDtZY&t=38s

Robbins, M. (2017, February 24). *https://fb.watch/3v-gxx1Qkh/* [Video]. Facebook. https://www.facebook.com/watch/?v=1224557697640112

Robbins, M. (2018). *The five elements of the 5 second rule.* Mel Robbins. https://melrobbins.com/five-elements-5-second-rule/

Segal, J., Smith, M., Segal, R., & Robinson, L. (2020). *Stress Symptoms, Signs, and Causes.* Help Guide. https://www.helpguide.org/articles/stress/stress-symptoms-signs-and-causes.htm#:~:text=Stress%20is%20your%20-body's%20way,body's%20way%20of%20protecting%20you

Selfstart. (n.d.). *The most important productivity habit: Breaking down and timing.* https://www.selfstart.co/articles/productivity/improve-productivity-by-breaking-down-tasks

Strusnik, B. (2018). *How I Eliminated Procrastination Forever and How You Can Too.* Medium. https://medium.com/benjaminstrusnik/how-i-eliminated-procrastination-forever-and-how-you-can-too-96466dd9dc96

Sugar Hill. (2020). *7 Ways Friends Influence Your Health As You Age.* SugarHill. https://resources.sugarhillrc.com/blog/people-around-affect

Swinder, B., Harari, D., Breidenthal, A. P., & Steed, L. B. (2018, December 27). *The Pros and Cons of Perfectionism,*

According to Research. HBR. https://hbr.org/2018/12/the-pros-and-cons-of-perfectionism-according-to-research

T, S. (n.d.). *Jeff Bezos | From a geek to an entrepreneur heading towards world domination.* Samarly. https://samarly. com/index.php/success-stories/jeff-bezos-success-story/

TedxTalks. (2019, November 21). *The Secret to Getting Anything You Want in Life given by Jennifer Cohen | Jen Cohen | TEDxBuckhead* [Video]. YouTube. https://www. youtube.com/watch?v=wM82hE6oimw

Tervooren, T. (n.d.). *27 Simple Tactics You Can Use Today to Become an Intrepid Risk-Taker.* Riskology. https://www. riskology.co/27-simple-tactics-you-can-use-today-to-become-an-intrepid-risk-taker/

Thaik, C. (2013). *Self-Doubt Destroys the Heart, Mind, Body and Soul.* Huffpost. https://www.huffpost.com/entry/self-doubt_b_2960936

Thelabb. (n.d.). *The Iceberg Illusion & Why Mistakes Matter.* https://www.thellabb.com/the-iceberg-illusion/

Tom Bilyeu. (2018, October 29). *If You Commit To Yourself, Here's What Will Happen* [Video]. YouTube. https://www. youtube.com/watch?v=K5PXiNpvfX0

Vicino, A. (2017). *The Psychology of Failure.* Medium. https://medium.com/swlh/the-psychology-of-failure-90eb0daf06da

Wabi-Sabi: How To Embrace This Ancient Japanese Philosophy At Home And Life? (2020). Japana Home. https://japanahome.com/journal/wabi-sabi-how-to-embrace-this-ancient-japanese-philosophy-at-home-and-life/

WebMd. (2020). *How stress Affects Your Health.* https://www.webmd.com/balance/stress-management/stress-anxiety-depression

Well, T. (2019). *Can You Be Too Self-Aware?* Psychology Today. https://www.psychologytoday.com/us/blog/the-clarity/201909/can-you-be-too-self-aware

What are the main mechanisms of homeostasis? (n.d.). Homeostasis Eleisha Biology. https://homeostasiseleishabiology.weebly.com/main-mechanisms-of-homeostasis.html

Wikipedia. (n.d.). *Rumination.* https://en.wikipedia.org/wiki/Rumination_(psychology)

Wilding, M. (2019). *How to make hypersensitivity your strongest skill at work.* QZ. https://qz.com/work/1762183/how-to-stop-overthinking-if-youre-a-highly-sensitive-person/

Winch, G. (2015). *10 Surprising Facts About Failure.* Psychology Today. https://www.psychologytoday.com/us/blog/the-squeaky-wheel/201501/10-surprising-facts-about-failure

Woods, L. (2018). *Jeff Bezos' Most Outrageous Business Failures*. Go Banking Rates. https://www.gobankingrates.com/money/business/jeff-bezos-worst-business-failures/#3

Young, K. (n.d.). *Remarkable New Research About Stress and the Brain. Hey Sigmund*. Hey Sigmund. https://www.heysigmund.com/new-research-on-stress-and-the-brain/

Printed in Great Britain
by Amazon

86638870R00099